Norman E. Gronlund
UNIVERSITY OF ILLINOIS

How to Write and Use Instructional Objectives

4th Edition

MACMILLAN PUBLISHING COMPANY
NEW YORK

COLLIER MACMILLAN CANADA
TORONTO

To
Marie Ann Gronlund
and
Erik, Derek, and David

Editor: Robert Miller
Production Supervisor: Elisabeth Fleshler
Production Manager: Valerie A. Sawyer
Text Design: Patrice Fodero and Blake Logan
Cover Design: Blake Logan

This book was set in Electra by Digitype, Inc.
The cover was printed by Phoenix Color Corp.

Macmillan Publishing Company
866 Third Avenue, New York, New York 10022

Collier Macmillan Canada, Inc.
1200 Eglinton Avenue East, Suite 200
Don Mills, Ontario M3C 3N1

Library of Congress Cataloging-in-Publication Data

Gronlund, Norman Edward, 1920–
     How to write and use instructional objectives / Norman E.
  Gronlund. — 4th ed.
        p.   cm.
     Rev. ed. of: Stating objectives for classroom instruction. 3rd ed.
  © 1985.
     Includes bibliographical references.
     ISBN 0-02-348001-7
     1. Lesson planning.   2. Education—Aims and objectives.
  I. Gronlund, Norman Edward, 1920–   Stating objectives for classroom
  instruction.   II. Title.
  LB1027.4.G76   1991   89-78446
     371.3'028—dc20   CIP
  Printing: 3 4 5 6 7   Year: 2 3 4 5 6 7

Preface

This is a practical guide that describes and illustrates how to write instructional objectives as intended learning outcomes and how to define the objectives in terms of student performance; that is, in terms of what students can do to demonstrate that they have achieved the objectives. When written in this way, objectives serve as a guide for teaching, testing, and the evaluation of learning.

Part I focuses on how to state instructional objectives so that they clearly convey instructional intent in terms of student performance. Self-checks are used throughout these chapters to enable students to evaluate their own level of understanding.

Part II describes the *Taxonomy of Educational Objectives* and how to write objectives for cognitive, affective, and performance outcomes. There is a separate chapter focusing on objectives for higher-level thinking skills.

Part III describes how to prepare a complete set of instructional objectives and how to use objectives in teaching, testing, and preparing evaluation instruments. The aim here is to show the role objectives play in the total instructional process and, thus, the importance of writing objectives as intended learning outcomes.

In addition to changing the organization of the book from the previous edition, several new chapters have been added:

- Chapter 5 Lower-Level Cognitive Outcomes
- Chapter 6 Higher-Level Thinking Skills
- Chapter 7 Affective Outcomes
- Chapter 8 Performance Outcomes

These new chapters describe and illustrate how to write instructional objectives in each of the areas indicated.

Other changes include the addition of new material to some chapters, new summaries, and the deletion of the chapter on marking and reporting. Although an area of concern for teachers, it was felt that marking and reporting was a more appropriate topic for a measurement textbook.

The approach to writing instructional objectives remains the same as earlier editions. It involves writing a set of general objectives and then defining each objective with a list of specific learning outcomes stated in terms of student performance. The procedure is useful at all levels of instruction, is applicable to all types of learning, and can be used to describe intended learning outcomes ranging from the simplest to the most complex.

After careful study of the material in this booklet, you should be able to:

1. Understand the importance of stating objectives as intended learning outcomes.
2. Understand the terms used in describing instructional objectives.
3. Judge whether an instructional objective has been properly stated as an intended learning outcome.
4. Judge whether an instructional objective has been adequately defined in terms of student performance.

5. Know the steps for identifying and defining a set of instructional objectives.
6. Understand the organization, content, and function of the *Taxonomy of Educational Objectives*.
7. Write instructional objectives for cognitive, affective, and performance outcomes.
8. Write a complete set of objectives for a course of instruction.
9. Recognize the role of instructional objectives in teaching at the "minimum-essentials level" and the "developmental level."
10. Recognize the role of instructional objectives in test preparation and item banking.
11. Recognize the role of instructional objectives in preparing evaluation instruments.
12. Evaluate a set of instructional objectives using a checklist of relevant criteria.

These general learning outcomes are most likely to be attained if reading of the material is supplemented by practice in identifying and defining instructional objectives.

My special thanks go to the individuals who reviewed the third edition and made many useful suggestions, to those who prepared the *Taxonomy of Educational Objectives*, to Calvin K. Claus for the list of verbs in Appendix B, to Robert Miller and the Macmillan editorial staff for their valuable help, and to Irene Palmer for her excellent typing.

N.E.G.

Contents

Part I

How to State Instructional Objectives

Chapter 1

Instructional Objectives as Intended Learning Outcomes

What Are Instructional Objectives?

In the past, instructional objectives have been stated in many different ways and have focused on various aspects of instruction (e.g., teaching procedures, learning process, instructional content, student behaviors). Here we shall describe instructional objectives as intended learning outcomes; that is, in terms of the types of performance students are able to demonstrate at the end of instruction to show that they have learned what was expected of them. Well-stated objectives clarify these expectations in terms of measurable or observable student performance.

In addition to focusing on the intended outcomes of instruction, instructional objectives must be at an appropriate level of generality for the type of instruction to be used. For classroom instruction they should not be stated so narrowly and detailed that instruction is reduced to a lock-step type of training program. Neither should they be in such generalized form that they provide inadequate guidance for instruction. Ideally, statements of instructional objectives should fall in the middle position on the generality continuum; that is, the statements should be specific enough to provide focus for both teaching and the evaluation of learning without limiting the teacher's flexibility in selecting instructional methods and materials. The ideal middle ground for stating instructional objectives can be illustrated as follows:

Too Narrow	Ideal	Too Broad
Lists of specific learning tasks students are able to do (e.g., adds two numbers that are less than 10)	Descriptions of expected student performance at the end of instruction (e.g., adds whole numbers)	Statements of general goals (e.g., develops proficiency in mathematics)

A list of specific tasks, such as those on the left end of the continuum, may be useful for programmed instruction, training programs, and some limited aspects of instruction. For most classroom instruction, however, they result in long unmanageable lists that neglect the integration and transfer of learning. Generalized statements, such as those on the right end, might serve well for policy making and program planning, but they are of little value for instructional purposes. What is needed for classroom instruction is a limited, manageable set of instructional objectives, with each objective defined by a list of the specific types of performance that students are able to demonstrate when they have achieved the objective. This procedure enables us to describe intended learning outcomes, ranging from simple to complex, and provides us the freedom to use a variety of instructional methods and materials to achieve the objectives.

Why Use Instructional Objectives?

Although much has been written about instructional objectives over the years, some teachers still ask this question. Numerous specific answers could be given, but basically they can be combined into the three purposes depicted below.

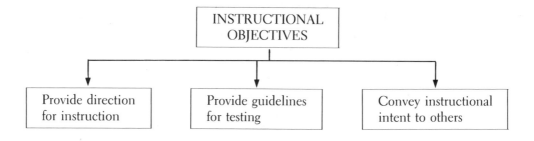

These purposes are best served, however, when the objectives are properly stated as intended learning outcomes of the instruction.

Focusing on Intended Learning Outcomes

There are, of course, many different ways of stating instructional objectives. One common type of statement is in terms of what we, as teachers, are going to do. Thus, we might have a statement like the following:

To demonstrate to students how to set up laboratory equipment.

The difficulty with a statement such as this is that it focuses attention on the teaching activity rather than on the learning outcomes to be attained by the students. Literally speaking, we have achieved the objective once we have completed the demonstration— whether or not the students have learned anything from it. A more fruitful way to state instructional objectives is in terms of the types of outcomes we expect from our teaching; therefore, after we demonstrate how to use laboratory equipment, we might expect students to be able to do the following:

1. Identify the laboratory equipment used in the demonstration.
2. Describe the steps to be followed in setting up the laboratory equipment.
3. List the necessary precautions in handling and setting up the laboratory equipment.
4. Demonstrate skills in setting up their own laboratory equipment.

When instructional objectives are stated like this, they direct attention to the students and to the types of performance students are expected to exhibit as a result of the learning experience. Our focus thus shifts from the teacher to the students and from the learning *process* to the learning *outcomes*. This shift clarifies the intent of our instruction and provides the basis for an evaluation of student learning.

The distinction between stating objectives in terms of what you are going to do as a teacher and stating them in terms of the learning outcomes you expect from your students is an important one. To check on your grasp of this distinction, look at the following two objectives and decide which one is stated as an expected learning outcome.[1]

1. Instills an understanding of the scientific method.
2. Distinguishes between valid and invalid conclusions.

You should have selected the second objective, which clearly specifies how students will demonstrate at the end of the instructional period that they have learned. Note that the statement begins with a verb that implies an activity on the part of the student. There is no need to add such refinements as "The student has the ability to *distinguish*," "The student can *distinguish*," or "The student should be able to demonstrate that he or she can *distinguish*." The less wordy the objective, the better. Our aim is to indicate clearly the intent of our instruction in terms of the type of response (*distinguishes between*) that the student is expected to show.

The word *instills* in the first statement implies that the teacher, not the student, is engaging in an activity. By omitting this word, you can restate this objective in terms of a learning outcome as follows:

Understands the scientific method.

Note that although this objective is now stated as an outcome, the term *understands* is much more general than the term *distinguishes between*. To indicate clearly the intent of our instruction, it would be necessary to further define this objective by listing the specific types of student performance we are willing to accept as evidence of their understanding (e.g., "explains the procedures," "describes the importance of controlling variables"). This process of stating general objectives and then of further defining them in terms of specific statements has some advantage over the use of single statements of objectives, as we shall see shortly. First, however, let's see if we can further clarify the meaning of "instructional objectives as intended learning outcomes" by taking a look at their role in the instructional process.

---

[1] Throughout Part I you will be presented with opportunities for self-testing. To benefit most, you should choose between alternatives before you continue your reading.

Learning Outcomes and the Instructional Process

The relation of learning outcomes to the learning experiences provided during the teaching–learning phase of instruction is shown in Figure 1.

Student $\rightarrow$	TEACHING–LEARNING PROCESS	$\rightarrow$	LEARNING OUTCOMES (End Products)
	(Learning experiences based on interaction of subject matter, teaching methods, and instructional materials)		Knowledge Understanding Application Thinking skills Performance skills Computer skills Communication skills Computational skills Work–study skills Social skills Attitudes Interests Appreciation Adjustments

FIGURE 1. Relation of learning outcomes to learning experiences.

This diagram makes clear the fact that the learning experiences provided during the teaching–learning process are not ends in themselves but means to ends. The subject matter, the teaching methods, and materials used in instruction are to be viewed as tools to bring about desired learning outcomes.

Although the diagram appears simple, the *process* of instruction and the *products* of instruction are frequently confused in statements of instructional objectives. For example, which one of the following objectives is stated as a *product* (i.e., a learning *outcome*)?

1. Increases proficiency in the use of charts and graphs.
2. Interprets charts and graphs.

You are correct if you selected the second objective, which describes in general terms what the student does at the end of the learning experience. We later would want to clarify further what we mean by *interprets* (e.g., identifies a given point on a graph, describes the trend shown in a graph), but this instructional objective is definitely stated as a learning *product*.

In the first statement the term *increases* provides a clue that we are concerned here with a *process*. The statement doesn't clarify how the student is to demonstrate his or her increased proficiency at the end of the instruction. Is the student to interpret charts and graphs, to construct charts and graphs, or to give a speech in which charts and graphs will be used as visual aids? Stating objectives in terms of the learning *process* is misleading because one learning experience may contribute to many different learning outcomes, and one learning outcome (e.g., a scientific attitude) may be the result of many different learning experiences.

The first step in instructional planning, then, should be to identify and define our instructional objectives as learning outcomes. When we specify the types of performance (i.e., knowledge, understanding, skills) that we expect students to be able to demonstrate at the end of instruction, we can more wisely select the materials and methods of instruction. The statements of intended outcomes also clarify the specific types of performance to be tested when evaluating student learning and can be used to convey our instructional intent to students, parents, and others who might be interested.

Stating Instructional Objectives as Intended Learning Outcomes

As noted earlier, there are two ways of stating objectives as learning outcomes. One is to list each specific type of performance students are to exhibit at the end of the instructional period. For example, we might start a list concerned with terminology as follows:

1. Defines the term in their own words.
2. Identifies the meaning of the term when used in context.
3. Distinguishes between terms that are similar in meaning.

A second method is to state first the general instructional objectives and then to clarify each objective by listing a *sample* of the specific types of student performance we are willing to accept as evidence of the attainment of that objective. This procedure would result in statements such as the following:

1. Understands the meaning of terms.
   1.1 Defines the term in their own words.
   1.2 Identifies the meaning of the term when used in context.
   1.3 Distinguishes between terms that are similar in meaning.

Note that the specific statements are the same in both instances. The first list, however, implies that these types of performance are ends in themselves and that instruction is to be given directly in the specified performance. For example, we teach students "to define a term in their own words"; then, to test achievement of the outcome, we ask them "to define the term in their own words." This one-to-one relationship between the performance taught and the performance tested is characteristic of the training level and is widely used in programmed instruction. For regular classroom instruction, however, this procedure is useful only for teaching the simplest skills and the lowest levels of knowledge.

Stating the general instructional objectives first and then clarifying it further by listing the specific types of performance that characterize the objective is more than a matter of literary form. This procedure makes clear that the instructional objective is *understanding* and not *defining, identifying,* or *distinguishing between.* These latter terms simply describe a *sample of the types of performance that represent understanding.* A different sample of specific types of performance could serve equally well. For example, we might use the following list instead of the one cited earlier.

1. Understands the meaning of terms.
    1.1 Relates terms to the concepts they represent.
    1.2 Uses each term in an original sentence.
    1.3 Identifies similarities and differences between terms.

Note that the instructional objective is still *understanding*. We have merely listed a new sample of student performance to characterize what is meant by the statement "Understands the meaning of terms." It would be impossible to list all types of performance that might show understanding; therefore, we must settle for a representative sample.

The particular sample of student performance that is selected to define an objective depends on both the level of instruction and the nature of the content. The general objective "Understands the meaning of terms" could be an appropriate learning outcome at the elementary, secondary, or college level. However, at the elementary level the sample of performance might consist of specific statements such as "identifies pictures of the term" (e.g., largest) and "follows directions indicated by the term" (e.g., add these numbers); whereas, at the high school or college level such specific outcomes as "describes the concept the term represents" and "uses the term correctly in stating a principle" may be more appropriate. Similarly, the specific sample of performance can vary somewhat with the subject being taught. For example, English teachers may find that statements such as "defines the term in their own words" and "uses the term in an original sentence" best clarify their intended outcomes, whereas science teachers may favor such statements as "distinguishes between terms" and "describes the process represented by the term." Thus, teachers at all levels and in various subject-matter areas might use some of the same general objectives, such as "Understands the meaning of terms," but each may describe the student performance they are willing to accept as evidence of understanding differently, depending on the level and nature of the instruction. Thus, it is the list of specific statements that describes the intended learning outcomes in terms of student performance. These are called *specific learning outcomes* (see Box 1.1).

The fact that specific learning outcomes simply serve as *samples* of the types of performance we are willing to accept as evidence of the attainment of our general instructional objectives has implications for both teaching and testing. Our teaching efforts must be directed toward the general objectives of instruction and not toward the specific samples of performance we have selected to represent each objective. For example, in teaching an *understanding of terms*, we might have the students study the textbook definitions, compare and contrast the terms during class discussion, and use the terms in oral and written work. When we test the students, however, we present them with a list of terms and ask them to define each term in their own words and to write an original sentence using the term. Note that the test calls for a type of response that was not directly taught during classroom instruction. This is necessary if the test results are to show an *understanding* rather than merely a *recall* of previous learning. Also, the test calls forth only a sample of the types of performance that might be used to represent an *understanding of terms*. It would be impractical to include test items that measure all aspects of understanding, just as it would be impractical to include all relevant terms in a particular test. In both cases we must be satisfied with a *sample*—a sample of the many terms that the students have

---

BOX 1.1 SOME BASIC TERMINOLOGY

General Instructional Objective	An intended outcome of instruction that has been stated in general enough terms to encompass a domain of student performance (e.g., "Comprehends the literal meaning of written material"). A general instructional objective must be further defined by a set of specific learning outcomes to clarify instructional intent.
Specific Learning Outcome	An intended outcome of instruction that has been stated in terms of specific and observable *student performance* (e.g., "Identifies details that are explicitly stated in a passage"). Specific learning outcomes describe the types of performance that learners will be able to exhibit when they have achieved a general instructional objective (specific learning outcomes are also called Specific Objectives, Performance Objectives, and Measurable Objectives).
Student Performance	Any measurable or observable student response that is a result of learning.

---

studied during instruction and a sample of the many types of performance that could be used as evidence of the student's understanding of terms. If our samples are carefully chosen, we can then generalize from our test results to the larger achievement domain. That is, we can estimate how well the students have achieved our instructional objective, the *understanding of terms*.

The method of stating objectives being described here does not include the *conditions* under which the performance is to be demonstrated nor the *standards* for determining a satisfactory level of performance. Although conditions and standards are sometimes included in statements of objectives, there are good reasons for not including them as part of the objective (see Box 1.2).

Summary

Instructional objectives are most useful for both teaching and the evaluation of student learning when stated as intended learning outcomes; that is, in terms of the types of performance students are able to demonstrate at the end of instruction to show that they have learned what was intended. When instruction is limited to simple learning tasks, as in a training program, it may be possible to list *all* of the types of performance involved in each task and to teach and test them directly. For classroom instruction, however, it is usually possible to list only a *sample* of the many specific types of performance that represent each instructional objective. These lists of specific learning outcomes provide a guide for both teaching and testing, but instruction should not focus on the sample of performance but rather on the larger achievement domain it represents. The necessity for sampling at higher levels of learning makes it desirable to define intended learning outcomes in two steps.

BOX 1.2 WHY NOT INCLUDE CONDITIONS AND STANDARDS?

It is sometimes suggested that in addition to describing the desired *student performance*, an objective should include the *conditions* under which the performance is to be demonstrated and the *standard* of performance to be accepted. This method of stating objectives would result in a statement as follows (each element is identified to the left of the statement):

Condition	Given a drawing of a flower
Performance	The student will label in writing
Standard	At least 4 of the 5 parts shown.

Statements such as this are especially useful for programmed instruction and for mastery testing in simple training programs. When used for regular classroom instruction, however, they result in long cumbersome lists that restrict the freedom of the teacher. If we restated the above as "Identifies the parts of a given plant structure," it could be used with various units of study and the teacher would be free to use real plants, pictures, diagrams, slides, or other stimulus material. Also, the students could respond orally, in writing, or simply by pointing to a named part. The standard (in this case 80%) could be set at the time of testing, either for the whole test or separately for each part. Keeping the standard separate from the objective makes it possible to vary the standards as needed without rewriting the objectives. For example, we may want to set lower standards at the beginning of a unit of study and higher standards at the end. Similarly we may want to set higher standards for a gifted group and lower standards for a retarded group. Let's not waste time rewriting objectives to fit changing conditions.

---

1. State the general instructional objectives as intended learning outcomes.
2. List under each objective a representative sample of the specific learning outcomes that indicate achievement of the objective.

The list of specific learning outcomes for each general instructional objective clarifies the types of performance students should be able to demonstrate when they have attained the objective. For any particular objective (e.g., "Understands terms"), the specific types of student performance can be expected to vary from one instructional level to another and from one content area to another. Thus, it is in the lists of specific learning outcomes that the objectives are made relevant to a particular instructional situation.

The conditions and standards of student performance should not be included in the statements of objectives. They can be considered separately at the time of student evaluation. This makes it possible to adjust the conditions and standards to fit changing situations without the rewriting of objectives.

Chapter 2

Stating the General Instructional Objectives

The first step in writing instructional objectives is to state the general learning outcomes we expect from our teaching. This step sounds simple enough, but most teachers find it difficult. They tend to focus on the teaching process, the learning process, or the subject matter, rather than on the expected *outcomes* of instruction. Teachers also have some difficulty stating the objectives at a satisfactory level of generality; that is, of striking a happy medium between broad, undefinable statements and long, unmanageable lists of specific types of behavior. Let's first take a look at some of the common errors to avoid in stating instructional objectives.

Avoiding Errors in Stating the General Objectives

One of the most common errors in stating objectives has already been considered—that of describing teacher performance rather than student performance. Look at the following two objectives, for example, and note the difference in how they are stated. Which one most clearly indicates an instructional outcome?

1. Comprehends assigned reading material.
2. To increase the student's reading ability.

You should have had little difficulty in selecting between these two statements. The first statement contains an expected outcome of instruction. Later we would need to list a sample of the specific types of performance that we are willing to accept as evidence that the student *comprehends*, but as stated this is a good general outcome.

The second statement offers a less clear picture of the intended results of instruction. It also gives the psychologically unsound impression that it is the teacher who is going to do the increasing rather than the student.

Another common error was also mentioned in Chapter 1; that is, stating an objective in terms of the learning *process* rather than as a learning *product*. The following two statements will clarify the difference. Which one is stated as a *product* of instruction, i.e., an instructional *outcome*?

1. Gains knowledge of basic principles.
2. Applies basic principles to new situations.

If you selected the second statement, you are correct. This statement clearly indicates what the student can do at the end of instruction. The first statement emphasizes the gaining of knowledge (learning *process*) rather than the type of performance that provides evidence that learning has taken place. Words like *gains, acquires,* and *develops* give away the fact that an objective is focused on the learning *process* rather than on the expected *outcome* of the learning experience.

In some cases where objectives are stated in terms of the learning *process*, the instructional intent is still fairly clear. This is frequently true for simple learning outcomes. For example, in the statement "Develops skill in adding whole numbers," the learning outcome is quite obvious. In other cases, however, a single learning experience might contribute to any number of learning outcomes, none of which is readily apparent in the statement of objectives. For example, look at the following statement.

Learns symbols on a weather map.

This statement does clarify what the student is to learn, but it does not clarify the learning *outcomes* toward which the student should be directed. The teacher who wrote this statement might have in mind any one of the following learning outcomes:

Recalls the symbols used on a weather map.

Identifies the symbols on a weather map.

Interprets a weather map (using the symbols).

Constructs a weather map (using the symbols).

Predicts weather from a weather map (using the symbols).

It is obvious that the statement "learns symbols" does not indicate the intent of the instruction so clearly as the statements of learning *outcomes* listed above. Identifying the nature of the desired product provides greater direction for planning, carrying out, and evaluating the learning experiences.

Another common error in stating objectives is simply to list the subject matter to be covered. This error is readily apparent in a comparison of the following two statements. Which one is properly stated?

1. Principles of electricity.
2. Understands basic principles.

The correct answer is, of course, the second statement. The first statement consists of no more than a subject-matter topic. There is no indication of what the students are expected to do with regard to the principles of electricity. Are students simply to know them, to understand them, or to apply them in some way?

The second statement could read "Understands principles of electricity," but there is some advantage in broadening the statement to include all types of principles covered in the instruction. The same outcome can then be used to indicate the expected reaction to any principle studied. When this is done, the specific types of student response used to clarify what is meant by the word *understands* must, of course, be *performance* oriented rather than *content* oriented. When complete, the statement of the objective and of the specific learning *outcomes* might appear as follows:

1. Understands basic principles.
   1.1 States the principle in his or her own words.
   1.2 Identifies an example of the principle.
   1.3 Distinguishes between correct and incorrect applications of the principle.
   1.4 Predicts an outcome based on the principle.

Note that the specific statements do not indicate what principles the students are to understand, but rather what *performance* they are to demonstrate as evidence that they understand. By not including a reference to subject matter in statements of learning *outcomes*, you can develop a set of outcomes that is useful with various units of instruction throughout a course. Thus the subject matter in each unit of instruction will indicate the principles that are to be studied, and the learning *outcomes* will indicate the types of reactions the students are to make to the principles.

Another common error is to include more than one type of learning *outcome* in each general objective. Look at the following two statements. Which one contains a *single outcome*?

1. Uses appropriate experimental procedures in solving problems.
2. Knows the scientific method and applies it effectively.

Of course the answer is 1. The second statement includes both *knows* and *applies* as possible *outcomes*. It is better to have a separate statement for each because some students may know the scientific method (i.e., be able to describe it) but may not be able to apply it effectively. With separate statements, you can define each objective in terms of specific learning outcomes and thus determine how well each objective is being achieved.

In this section we have focused on the common errors to avoid in stating the general instructional objectives. These errors include stating the objectives in terms of (1) the teacher's performance, (2) the learning process, (3) the subject matter, and (4) a combination of two or more outcomes. These errors can be avoided by *focusing attention on the student and on the type of performance he or she is expected to demonstrate at the end of instruction*. Instructional objectives, then, should be brief, clear statements that describe instructional intent in terms of the desired learning *outcomes* (see Box 2.1).

In addition to avoiding the common errors in stating instructional objectives, one of the most difficult tasks is to select the proper level of generality in stating each major objective.

BOX 2.1 STATING INSTRUCTIONAL OBJECTIVES

1. Don't state them in terms of *teacher performance*. (e.g., Teach students scientific concepts.)
2. Don't state them in terms of the *learning process*. (e.g., Student learns scientific concepts.)
3. Don't focus on the *subject-matter* topics. (e.g., Student learns the meaning of osmosis, photosynthesis, etc.)
4. Don't include two objectives in one statement. (e.g., Student knows and understands scientific concepts.)

State and define each objective in terms of the type of *student performance* that is to be demonstrated at the end of instruction, as illustrated below:

1. Understands scientific concepts.

   1.1 Defines the concept.

   1.2 Identifies an example of the concept.

   1.3 States hypotheses based on the concept.

   1.4 Describes how the process functions in a given situation.

   1.5 Describes an experiment that illustrates the process.

Selecting the Proper Level of Generality

When developing a list of general instructional objectives for a course (or unit of course work), our aim is to obtain a list of outcomes to work toward and not a list of specific tasks to be performed by all students. To be sure, each general instructional objective will need to be defined further by a sample of the specific types of student performance that characterize each objective, but at this stage we are focusing only on the stating of the general objectives.

You may have noticed by now that each of the instructional objectives used in this chapter to illustrate properly stated learning outcomes began with a verb. The following verbs were used in these statements.

Applies

Comprehends

Knows

Understands

Uses

These verbs provide a clue to the desired level of generality for our major objectives. They are specific enough to provide direction for instruction without overly restricting the teacher or reducing the instruction to the training level. They are also specific enough to be easily defined by a brief list of the types of performance students are to demonstrate when the objectives have been achieved.

Let's look at a few sample statements that illustrate the problem of selecting a proper level of generality. Which one of the following statements represents the most general objective? Which one the most specific?

1. Communicates effectively in English.
2. Writes clear, effective English.
3. Punctuates sentences properly.

The first statement represents the most general objective. In fact, it is probably too general for a major objective because communication includes speaking, listening,

---

BOX 2.2 SOME SAMPLE GENERAL INSTRUCTIONAL OBJECTIVES

READING

1. Knows word meanings.
2. Comprehends the literal meaning of written material.
3. Infers meaning from written material.
4. Interprets tables, graphs, maps, and diagrams.
5. Evaluates written material using specific criteria (e.g., realistic, accurate).
6. Adapts reading rate to material and purpose of reading.
7. Locates information by using guides (e.g., index, table of contents, reference works).
8. Demonstrates a positive attitude toward reading.

MATHEMATICS

1. Knows the meaning of terms and symbols.
2. Computes accurately and rapidly.
3. Understands mathematical concepts and processes.
4. Understands the number systems.
5. Applies concepts and processes to mathematical problems.
6. Invents new mathematical applications or generalizations.
7. Interprets measuring instruments, tables, and graphs.
8. Demonstrates a positive attitude toward mathematics.

SCIENCE

1. Knows the meaning of terms.
2. Knows specific facts.
3. Knows laboratory procedures.
4. Understands concepts and principles.
5. Applies concepts and principles to new situations.
6. Demonstrates skills and abilities needed to conduct an experiment.
7. Interprets data in scientific reports.
8. Displays a scientific attitude.

writing, and reading. Each of these areas is general enough to provide a major objective by itself.

The most specific is 3, which might be a good specific learning outcome to be listed under a more general objective, but it is probably too specific to be used as a general instructional objective. Thus the second statement comes closest to the desired level of generality. It clearly indicates the general nature of the expected learning *outcome*, and it can be defined by a relatively short, clear list of specific learning outcomes.

The degree of generality in the list of major objectives will, of course, vary with the period of instruction for which the list is being prepared. The objectives for an entire course will, of necessity, be more general than those for a unit of instruction within the course. Teachers typically find that from eight to twelve general instructional objectives are sufficient for a course of instruction and from two to four for a brief instructional unit (see Box 2.2).

Summary

Use the following suggestions as a guide for stating the general instructional objectives.

1. State each general instructional objective as an *intended learning outcome* (i.e., students' *terminal performance*).
2. Begin each general objective with a verb that is general enough to encompass a domain of student performance (e.g., *knows*, *understands*, *applies*). Omit "The student is able to. . . ."
3. State each general objective so that it includes only one general learning outcome, rather than combining several outcomes.
4. Keep the statements relatively free of *specific* subject matter so they can be used with various instructional units.
5. State each general objective at a level of generality that is readily definable by a set of specific learning outcomes. Including from eight to twelve general instructional objectives for a course of instruction will usually suffice. For a brief unit of instruction, from two to four general objectives may be enough.

Chapter 3

Stating the Specific Learning Outcomes

When you have prepared a tentative list of general instructional objectives, you are ready to define each general objective in terms of the specific types of student performance that you are willing to accept as evidence that the objective has been achieved. These *specific learning outcomes* provide an operational definition of what we mean when we state that a student "knows terms," "understands principles," or "interprets charts and graphs." Unless the general objectives are further clarified in this way, they will convey only a fuzzy notion of the intended outcomes of instruction.

Stating the Specific Outcomes in Terms of Student Performance

The following statement of a general instructional objective and list of specific learning outcomes illustrates what is meant by defining instructional objectives in terms of *student performance*.

1. Knows specific facts (American History).
   1.1 Identifies important dates, events, places, and persons.
   1.2 Describes the characteristics of a given historical period.
   1.3 Lists important events in chronological order.
   1.4 Relates events to their most probable causes.

Note that each specific learning outcome starts with an *action verb* that indicates *observable* student responses; that is, responses that can be seen by an outside observer.

These verbs are listed as follows in order to clarify the types of terms needed for stating the specific learning outcomes.

Identifies

Describes

Lists

Relates

These verbs describe the types of responses the students are to exhibit as evidence that they have achieved the general instructional objective "Knows specific facts." As noted earlier, these responses provide only a sample of the specific outcomes that could be included under this objective. The list might be lengthened, shortened, or radically modified to fit the emphasis of a particular course. As an instructor you must define your own instructional objectives in terms of the specific learning outcomes you deem most appropriate. All we are doing here is illustrating the process of stating the specific outcomes in terms of identifiable student performance.

To check on your ability to distinguish between appropriate and inappropriate terms, look at the following two statements. Which one is stated in terms of student performance?

1. Realizes the importance of neatness.
2. Explains the importance of neatness.

You are correct if you selected the second statement. The term "explains" indicates a response that is definite and clearly observable. The first statement does not specify how students will demonstrate that they *realize* the importance of neatness. Will they give reasons for being neat or will they dress more neatly? Terms such as this are subject to many interpretations and should be avoided when you state the specific learning outcomes for each general objective. Let's try another pair of statements to be sure you can tell the difference between *performance* and *nonperformance* terms. Which one of the following clearly indicates student performance?

1. Predicts the outcome of an experiment.
2. Sees the value of an experiment.

This time you should have had little difficulty in selecting the first statement as the correct answer. The term "sees" is a common one in education (e.g., "I see the point"), and its familiarity might have misled you. But, note that "sees" refers to an internal state. What will the students do when they see the value of an experiment? Will they describe its usefulness, point out its theoretical implications, or estimate the social consequences of the results? We simply can't tell because the term "sees" is vague, indefinite, and describes a reaction that is not directly observable.

In stating specific learning outcomes, then, it is wise to begin each statement with a verb that specifies definite, observable student performance. Statements beginning with a verb clarify from the outset the types of responses students are expected to make when they have achieved the general objective. Helpful lists of verbs for stating specific learning outcomes are included in Appendix B.

Obtaining a Representative Sample
of Specific Learning Outcomes

When defining a general objective with a list of specific learning outcomes, you will need to decide how many specific outcomes to list for each objective. There are no hard-and-fast rules for this. It is obvious that simple knowledge and skill outcomes will require fewer than more complex ones, but even relatively simple instructional objects may encompass such a large number of specific types of performance that only a small proportion of them can be listed. Take "knowledge of terms," for example, and note the various types of student performance that might be listed.

1. Knows the meaning of terms.
    1.1 Writes a definition of the term.
    1.2 Identifies a definition of the term.
    1.3 Identifies the term that fits a given description.
    1.4 Identifies a synonym of the term.
    1.5 Identifies an antonym of the term.
    1.6 Identifies an example of the term.
    1.7 Identifies the term represented by a symbol (e.g., +, −).
    1.8 Draws a picture that represents the term (e.g., circle, square).
    1.9 Describes the procedure the term represents.
    1.10 States the concept or principle that fits the term.
    1.11 Describes the relationship of the term to a second term.
    1.12 Differentiates between the term and a second term.
    1.13 Differentiates between the technical meaning and the common meaning of the term.
    1.14 Identifies the best meaning of the term when used in a sentence.
    1.15 Distinguishes between proper and improper usage of the term.

Although this list is not exhaustive, it makes clear the futility of attempting to list all of the possible specific types of responses that might represent a particular objective. All we can reasonably expect to do is to list a sample of the specific types of performance that the students are expected to demonstrate when they have achieved the objective. The aim is to select as representative a sample as possible, so that students' performance on the selected outcomes will be characteristic of what their performance would be like on similar outcomes encompassed by the same general instructional objective.

The specific outcomes that are most representative of a general instructional objective will be modified by both the nature of the subject taught and the grade level at which the instruction is given. For "Knowing terms," for example, a reading teacher would be likely to stress the identification of synonyms, antonyms, the meaning of words in context, and similar outcomes related to reading ability; whereas, a math teacher would emphasize outcomes that relate the meaning of terms to symbols (e.g., ×, =), figures (e.g., types of angles), operations (e.g., grouping into *sets*), and the like. Similarly, a primary teacher would be likely to state fewer and simpler types of outcomes based on picture identification and student drawings.

When the instructional objectives are *complex*, special care is needed to ensure that all key elements are included. To identify the key elements in complex objectives, it is often necessary to consult reference books and other relevant materials. You are not likely to find a neat list of outcomes from which to choose, but even general discussions of the concepts involved will help to define the objectives. Thus, when objectives are concerned with *thinking skills*, *scientific inquiry*, and the like, a trip to the library might be needed.

Complex objectives are difficult to define but are usually more important from an educational standpoint. Don't overload your list of instructional objectives with simple learning outcomes simply because they are easy to define.

Emphasizing Instructional Intent

The *action verb* is the key element in stating the specific learning outcomes that define each general instructional objective. The selection of action verbs thus is a vital step in the preparation of a useful set of objectives. In general, we should select those verbs that (1) most clearly convey our instructional intent and (2) most precisely specify the student performance we are willing to accept as evidence that the general instructional objective has been achieved. Unfortunately, action verbs vary widely in their ability to meet both criteria.

Some verbs communicate instructional intent well but are less precise concerning the specific response to be observed. Other verbs clearly indicate the performance to be observed, but the indicated response does not satisfactorily convey the intent of the instruction. Let's look at a few examples. Which one of the following most clearly conveys instructional intent? Which one most precisely specifies the performance to be observed?

1. Identifies the parts on a diagram for an electrical circuit.
2. Labels the parts on a diagram for an electrical circuit.

If you selected the first statement as most clearly conveying instructional intent, you are correct. In this particular instance, the focus of our instruction would be on the *identification* of the parts and not the labeling of them. Although the term "labels" is more descriptive of the precise response the students are expected to make, labeling is not the intended learning outcome. We assume students already know how to label. In this instance, we are simply using labeling as one way that identification might be shown. Identification might also be shown by pointing to, touching, marking, matching, circling, underlining, and so on. These *indicators* of "the ability to identify" clearly specify the student performance to be observed, but they do not always make clear the intent of the instruction.

Given a choice between verbs that clearly convey instructional intent and those that merely serve as performance indicators, it is wise to select the former when stating specific learning outcomes. For test construction purposes, it may be desirable to include both by adding a third level of specificity to the set of intended learning outcomes (see Box 3.1).

BOX 3.1 USING THREE LEVELS TO SPECIFY INTENDED LEARNING OUTCOMES

1. Comprehends the meaning of written material.

   1.1 Identifies information that is explicitly stated in a passage.

      1.11 Underlines specific details in the passage (e.g., names, dates, events).

      1.12 Selects statements that best match the literal meaning of the passage.

      1.13 Lists facts that support the major theme of the passage.

   1.2 Identifies the main thought of a passage.

      1.21 Underlines the topic sentence in the passage.

      1.22 Selects the best title for the passage.

   1.3 Summarizes the ideas in a passage.

      1.31 Writes a condensed version of the passage.

   1.4 Infers ideas and relationships not explicitly stated in a passage.

      1.41 Describes ideas, actions, or events that are implied in the content of the passage.

      1.42 Lists actions or events in the order in which they most likely occurred.

      1.43 Selects the most probable outcome for an action or event that is described in the passage.

      1.44 Explains why objects, ideas, or events should be grouped together.

Clarifying Intent with Sample Test Items

For some purposes it may be desirable to clarify specific learning outcomes with sample test items. This is especially useful where the outcomes are to serve as a basis for test construction by a group of teachers (e.g., for a department test). Nothing communicates the expected student response to others so precisely as sample test items. For example, specific outcomes for "knowing terms" might be further clarified as follows:

OUTCOME: IDENTIFIES A DEFINITION OF THE TERM

1. What is meant by *overt behavior*?

  *A. Behavior that is observable by others.

  B. Behavior that is repeated over and over again.

  C. Behavior that occurs within an individual.

  D. Misbehavior that should be corrected.

OUTCOME: IDENTIFIES A SYNONYM OF THE TERM

2. Which of the following terms has the same meaning as *create*?

    A. Acquire

    B. Alter

    C. Initiate

    *D. Originate

OUTCOME: IDENTIFIES AN ANTONYM OF THE TERM

3. Which one of the following terms means the opposite of *expand*?

    *A. Contract

    B. Divide

    C. Enlarge

    D. Extend

* Correct answer

Each sample test item clarifies what is meant by the specific outcome and serves as a model for constructing test items that call forth the intended student response.

Keeping the Statements Relatively Free of Course Content

As with the general instructional objectives, the specific learning outcomes should be kept free of *specific* course content. The following statements, for example, would be too content oriented.

Identifies the parts of the heart.

Identifies the parts of the lung.

Describes the functions of the heart.

Describes the functions of the lung.

For most classroom purposes, it would be more desirable to state the specific learning outcomes as follows:

Identifies the parts of a given structure.

Describes the functions of a given structure.

Statements like these clearly describe what type of performance the students are to demonstrate, but the responses are not tied to a specific body part. In fact, the revised statements would be useful with any animal or plant structure we are studying. The advantage of keeping the statements content free is, of course, that a set of objectives can then be used with various units of study. The subject-matter topics in each unit specify the content the student is to react to, and the specific learning outcomes describe the types of reactions to be made by the students.

To be sure you grasp this distinction, look at the following pair of learning outcomes and decide which one would be most useful with various units of study.

Lists the major battles of World War II in chronological order.

Lists historical events in chronological order.

It is rather obvious that the second one is a common learning outcome that can be used repeatedly in a history course. This statement also illustrates that keeping the stated outcomes content free is a matter of degree. Sometimes all we need to do is substitute generalized content (e.g., historical events) for specific content (e.g., World War II). Thus, when we find ourselves listing specific tasks such as the following, we might simply combine them into a single statement like "Distinguishes among geometric shapes."

Distinguishes between a circle and a square.

Distinguishes between a square and a rectangle.

Distinguishes between a rectangle and a triangle.

There is nothing basically wrong with combining the student responses and specific course content in the same statement. In fact, it would probably be desirable when preparing materials for programmed instruction or when dealing with some limited type of training program. However, when used for regular classroom instruction, the inclusion of specific course content in each statement results in the repetitious writing of objectives as each new subject-matter topic is considered. This time might be better spent in developing instructional materials, in preparing valid tests, and in doing other instructional tasks.

Making Sure the Specific Learning Outcomes Are Relevant

It goes without saying that each specific learning outcome should be relevant to the instructional objective it is defining, but this criterion constitutes another area of difficulty in listing the specific statements. Look at the following two statements, for example. Which one should be listed under the general goal "Understands scientific principles"?

1. Makes a prediction using the principle.
2. States the textbook definition of the principle.

Given a choice between these two, we would have to select the first. The second statement implies no more than the simple recall of information and therefore would be best classified as a *knowledge* outcome. The first statement goes beyond the recall of previously learned facts and asks the student to use the principle in a way that reflects an understanding of its meaning.

The problem is not quite that simple, however. Since knowledge is a prerequisite to understanding, there may be a tendency to list the specific types of performance for both under any objective concerned with understanding. Although this practice might appear sensible at first glance, it should generally be avoided. If it were carried to an extreme, for example, the most complex objective would have to include all of the specific types of performance listed under all of the other objectives. It is much better to define each instructional objective with the specific types of performance that are unique to that particular objective. When we define "knowledge of principles" and "understanding of principles" separately, for example, we are then able to identify those students who can demonstrate achievement of the knowledge outcomes but not those of understanding. This enhances the diagnostic value of the objectives for both teaching and testing.

Revising the General Objectives as Needed

During the process of defining the general instructional objectives, it may be necessary to modify the original list. In identifying the specific learning outcomes for the objectives, you may realize that some of them are too general and need to be subdivided. An objective on *problem solving* in arithmetic, for example, might better express instructional intent if it is broken down into *computational skill* and *solving story problems*. In defining other objectives, you might note that the specific learning outcomes overlap to such a degree that it is desirable to combine two statements into a single objective. Thus, "applies scientific procedures" and "plans simple experiments" might best be combined into a single objective such as "Uses the scientific method effectively." Because instructional objectives can be stated in many different ways and at various levels of generality, there is considerable flexibility in the formulation of the statements. The listing of the specific learning outcomes thus provides a good opportunity for evaluating the original list of instructional objectives and for revising them as necessary. The ultimate aim, of course, is to derive a final list of general objectives and specific learning outcomes that most clearly indicates your instructional intent.

Summary of Steps for Defining Instructional Objectives

In general summary, the procedure for defining instructional objectives in terms of student performance includes the following steps.

1. State the general instructional objectives as *expected learning outcomes*.
2. Place under each general instructional objective a list of specific learning outcomes that describes the *terminal performance* students are to demonstrate when they have achieved the *objective*.
    a. Begin each specific learning outcome with a *verb* that specifies definite *observable performance* and conveys *instructional intent*.
    b. List a *representative sample* of specific learning outcomes under each objective to adequately describe the performance of students who have achieved the objective.
    c. Add a third level of specificity to the list of outcomes, or illustrate with sample test items, if needed.
    d. Keep the specific learning outcomes relatively free of course content so that the list can be used with different units of study.
    e. Be certain that each specific learning outcome is *relevant* to the objective it describes.

3. When defining the general instructional objectives in terms of specific learning outcomes, revise and refine the original list of objectives as needed.

4. Be careful not to omit complex objectives (e.g., thinking skills) simply because they are difficult to define in terms of specific learning outcomes.

5. Consult reference materials for help in identifying the specific types of performance that are most appropriate for defining the complex objectives.

Part II

Writing Instructional Objectives in Various Areas

Chapter 4

Using the Taxonomy of Educational Objectives

One of the most helpful guides in identifying and defining instructional objectives is the *Taxonomy of Educational Objectives*, developed by committees under the direction of Bloom (1956) and Krathwohl (1964). The *Taxonomy* provides a classification of educational objectives that is analogous to the classification scheme used for plants and animals. It consists of a set of general and specific categories that encompass all possible learning outcomes that might be expected from instruction. The classification system was developed by psychologists, teachers, and test experts for use in curriculum development, teaching, and testing. Because the system is based on the assumption that learning outcomes can be best described in terms of changes in student performance, it is especially useful to teachers who are attempting to state their instructional objectives in performance terms.

The *Taxonomy* is divided into three main parts: (1) the cognitive domain, (2) the affective domain, and (3) the psychomotor domain. The cognitive domain includes those objectives that emphasize intellectual outcomes, such as knowledge, understanding, and thinking skills. The affective domain includes those objectives that emphasize feeling and emotion, such as interests, attitudes, appreciation, and methods of adjustment. The psychomotor domain includes those objectives that emphasize motor skills, such as handwriting, typing, swimming, and operating machinery. A complete classification system was developed for the cognitive and affective domains by the Bloom and Krathwohl committees, but the preparation of the psychomotor domain was never completed. In recent years, however, at least two major classification systems for the psychomotor domain have been prepared, neither one by the original taxonomy developers. We shall present one of these psychomotor systems for illustrative purposes.

The Cognitive and Affective Domains

The cognitive and affective domains have the most highly developed and detailed classification systems. The categories and subcategories in each of these domains are arranged in hierarchical order, from the simplest outcomes to the most complex. The cognitive domain, for example, starts with simple knowledge outcomes and then proceeds through the increasingly complex levels of comprehension, application, analysis, synthesis, and evaluation. Each category is assumed to include the behavior at the lower levels. Thus, comprehension includes the behavior at the knowledge level; application includes that at both the knowledge and comprehension levels, and so on. The affective domain follows a similar hierarchical pattern, ranging from the simple receiving of stimuli to the development of a value system that characterizes an individual's life style.

On following pages, in Tables I and III, are brief descriptions of each of the major categories in the cognitive and affective domains. Accompanying Tables (II and IV) also present examples of objectives and illustrative verbs for stating the specific learning outcomes for each of the categories. These examples should help clarify the meaning of each category and suggest types of learning outcomes to consider when identifying and defining instructional objectives. The illustrative objectives are not exhaustive, of course, but a review of them should stimulate you to think of a broader range of objectives for your particular area of instruction.

The list of verbs for each taxonomy category is only a sample of some of the more relevant action verbs. It must also be kept in mind that frequently the same term may be appropriately used at several levels. The term "identifies," for example, is appropriate in each of the following cases:

Knowledge:	Identifies the correct definition of the term.
Understanding:	Identifies examples of the principle.
Application:	Identifies proper grammar usage.
Analysis:	Identifies the parts of a sentence.

Despite this considerable overlap in the use of terms, there are some action verbs that are more directly relevant to one taxonomy category than to another. Those listed in the tables are merely suggestive; but they can assist in selecting the terms that most clearly convey the instructional intent of a given objective. More comprehensive lists of action verbs for stating specific learning are presented in Appendix B.

If you would like more elaborate and detailed treatments of the cognitive and affective domains, see the handbooks by Bloom (1956) and Krathwohl (1964) in the list of references in Appendix C. Both books provide extensive descriptions of the major and minor categories, with numerous illustrative objectives and test items. In reviewing these guides, you will find that the illustrative objectives are not stated in the way that we are advocating in this book. They are more general, are not defined by specific learning outcomes, and contain more subject-matter content than we are suggesting. However, they do provide excellent classification systems and a wealth of useful ideas for preparing and organizing a list of instructional objectives.

The Psychomotor Domain

The psychomotor domain is concerned with motor skills. Although this domain includes some learning outcomes that are common to most subjects (writing, speaking, laboratory skills), it receives major emphasis in commercial subjects, health sciences, home economics, industrial education, physical education, art, and music.

The classification system for the psychomotor domain that is shown in Table V is one developed by Simpson (1972). It was selected for use because the categories seem appropriate for classifying a wide variety of different types of motor skills. The major categories, ranging from perception (the lowest level) to origination (the highest level), have a hierarchical arrangement similar to that in the cognitive and affective domains. As with the other two domains, illustrative objectives and relevant action verbs are presented for each category (see Table VI).

A taxonomy in the psychomotor domain has also been developed by Harrow (1972). Her taxonomy seems to be especially well adapted to the area of physical education but may prove useful in other areas as well.

Instructional objectives in the psychomotor domain typically include concomitant cognitive and affective elements, but the demonstration of a motor skill is the dominant characteristic of the student's response. This overlapping of behavior from the different domains is, of course, not limited to performance skills. Learning outcomes in the cognitive area have some affective elements, and outcomes in the affective area have some cognitive components. The three domains of the *Taxonomy* provide a useful classification system, but they simply represent particular emphases in stating objectives and not mutually exclusive divisions.

Summary

The *Taxonomy of Educational Objectives* provides a three-domain scheme (cognitive, affective, and psychomotor) for classifying all possible instructional objectives. Each domain is subdivided into a series of categories that are arranged in hierarchical order— from simple to complex. A review of these categories and the illustrative objectives and action verbs accompanying them (Tables I to VI) should aid in (1) identifying objectives for a particular instructional unit, (2) stating objectives at the proper level of generality, (3) defining objectives in the most relevant terms, (4) checking on the comprehensiveness of a list of objectives, and (5) communicating to others the nature and level of learning outcomes included in a list of objectives.

As useful as the *Taxonomy* may be, don't become a slave to the system of classification. Some objectives will include elements of all three taxonomy domains. Such objectives should not be discarded simply because they are difficult to classify. Use the taxonomy domains only as a guide.

TABLE I. Major Categories in the Cognitive Domain of the Taxonomy of Educational Objectives (Bloom, 1956)

Descriptions of the Major Categories in the Cognitive Domain

1. Knowledge. Knowledge is defined as the remembering of previously learned material. This may involve the recall of a wide range of material, from specific facts to complete theories, but all that is required is the bringing to mind of the appropriate information. Knowledge represents the lowest level of learning outcomes in the cognitive domain.

2. Comprehension. Comprehension is defined as the ability to grasp the meaning of material. This may be shown by translating material from one form to another (words to numbers), by interpreting material (explaining or summarizing), and by estimating future trends (predicting consequences or effects). These learning outcomes go one step beyond the simple remembering of material, and represent the lowest level of understanding.

3. Application. Application refers to the ability to use learned material in new and concrete situations. This may include the application of such things as rules, methods, concepts, principles, laws, and theories. Learning outcomes in this area require a higher level of understanding than those under comprehension.

4. Analysis. Analysis refers to the ability to break down material into its component parts so that its organizational structure may be understood. This may include the identification of the parts, analysis of the relationships between parts, and recognition of the organizational principles involved. Learning outcomes here represent a higher intellectual level than comprehension and application because they require an understanding of both the content and the structural form of the material.

5. Synthesis. Synthesis refers to the ability to put parts together to form a new whole. This may involve the production of a unique communication (theme or speech), a plan of operations (research proposal), or a set of abstract relations (scheme for classifying information). Learning outcomes in this area stress creative behaviors, with major emphasis on the formulation of *new* patterns of structures.

6. Evaluation. Evaluation is concerned with the ability to judge the value of material (statement, novel, poem, research report) for a given purpose. The judgments are to be based on definite criteria. These may be internal criteria (organization) or external criteria (relevance to the purpose), and the student may determine the criteria or be given them. Learning outcomes in this area are highest in the cognitive hierarchy because they contain elements of all of the other categories, plus conscious value judgments based on clearly defined criteria.

TABLE II. Examples of General Instructional Objections and Clarifying Verbs for the Cognitive Domain of the Taxonomy

Illustrative General Instructional Objectives	Illustrative Verbs for Stating Specific Learning Outcomes
Knows common terms Knows specific facts Knows methods and procedures Knows basic concepts Knows principles	Defines, describes, identifies, labels, lists, matches, names, outlines, reproduces, selects, states
Understands facts and principles Interprets verbal material Interprets charts and graphs Translates verbal material to mathematical formulas Estimates future consequences implied in data Justifies methods and procedures	Converts, defends, distinguishes, estimates, explains, extends, generalizes, gives examples, infers, paraphrases, predicts, rewrites, summarizes
Applies concepts and principles to new situations Applies laws and theories to practical situations Solves mathematical problems Constructs charts and graphs Demonstrates correct usage of a method or procedure	Changes, computes, demonstrates, discovers, manipulates, modifies, operates, predicts, prepares, produces, relates, shows, solves, uses
Recognizes unstated assumptions Recognizes logical fallacies in reasoning Distinguishes between facts and inferences Evaluates the relevancy of data Analyzes the organizational structure of a work (art, music, writing)	Breaks down, diagrams, differentiates, discriminates, distinguishes, identifies, illustrates, infers, outlines, points out, relates, selects, separates, subdivides
Writes a well-organized theme Gives a well-organized speech Writes a creative short story (or poem, or music) Proposes a plan for an experiment Integrates learning from different areas into a plan for solving a problem Formulates a new scheme for classifying objects (or events, or ideas)	Categorizes, combines, compiles, composes, creates, devises, designs, explains, generates, modifies, organizes, plans, rearranges, reconstructs, relates, reorganizes, revises, rewrites, summarizes, tells, writes
Judges the logical consistency of written material Judges the adequacy with which conclusions are supported by data Judges the value of a work (art, music, writing) by use of internal criteria Judges the value of a work (art, music, writing) by use of external standards of excellence	Appraises, compares, concludes, contrasts, criticizes, describes, discriminates, explains, justifies, interprets, relates, summarizes, supports

TABLE III. Major Categories in the Affective Domain of the Taxonomy of Educational
Objectives (Krathwohl, 1964)

Descriptions of the Major Categories in the Affective Domain

1. Receiving. Receiving refers to the student's willingness to attend to particular phenomena or stimuli (classroom activities, textbook, music, etc.). From a teaching standpoint, it is concerned with getting, holding, and directing the student's attention. Learning outcomes in this area range from the simple awareness that a thing exists to selective attention on the part of the learner. Receiving represents the lowest level of learning outcomes in the affective domain.

2. Responding. Responding refers to active participation on the part of the student. At this level he or she not only attends to a particular phenomenon but also reacts to it in some way. Learning outcomes in this area may emphasize acquiescence in responding (reads assigned material), willingness to respond (voluntarily reads beyond assignment), or satisfaction in responding (reads for pleasure or enjoyment). The higher levels of this category include those instructional objectives that are commonly classified under "interest"; that is, those that stress the seeking out and enjoyment of particular activities.

3. Valuing. Valuing is concerned with the worth or value a student attaches to a particular object, phenomenon, or behavior. This ranges in degree from the more simple acceptance of a value (desires to improve group skills) to the more complex level of commitment (assumes responsibility for the effective functioning of the group). Valuing is based on the internalization of a set of specified values, but clues to these values are expressed in the student's overt behavior. Learning outcomes in this area are concerned with behavior that is consistent and stable enough to make the value clearly identifiable. Instructional objectives that are commonly classified under "attitudes" and "appreciation" would fall into this category.

4. Organization. Organization is concerned with bringing together different values, resolving conflicts between them, and beginning the building of an internally consistent value system. Thus the emphasis is on comparing, relating, and synthesizing values. Learning outcomes may be concerned with the conceptualization of a value (recognizes the responsibility of each individual for improving human relations) or with the organization of a value system (develops a vocational plan that satisfies his or her need for both economic security and social service). Instructional objectives relating to the development of a philosophy of life would fall into this category.

5. Characterization by a Value or Value Complex. At this level of the affective domain the individual has a value system that has controlled his or her behavior for a sufficiently long time for him or her to have developed a characteristic "life-style." Thus the behavior is pervasive, consistent, and predictable. Learning outcomes at this level cover a broad range of activities, but the major emphasis is on the fact that the behavior is typical or characteristic of the student. Instructional objectives that are concerned with the student's general patterns of adjustment (personal, social, emotional) would be appropriate here.

TABLE IV. Examples of General Instructional Objectives and Clarifying Verbs for the Affective Domain of the Taxonomy

Illustrative General Instructional Objectives	Illustrative Verbs for Stating Specific Learning Outcomes
Listens attentively Shows awareness of the importance of learning Shows sensitivity to human needs and social problems Accepts differences of race and culture Attends closely to the classroom activities	Asks, chooses, describes, follows, gives, holds, identifies, locates, names, points to, replies, selects, sits erect, uses
Completes assigned homework Obeys school rules Participates in class discussion Completes laboratory work Volunteers for special tasks Shows interest in subject Enjoys helping others	Answers, assists, complies, conforms, discusses, greets, helps, labels, performs, practices, presents, reads, recites, reports, selects, tells, writes
Demonstrates belief in the democratic process Appreciates good literature (art or music) Appreciates the role of science (or other subjects) in everyday life Shows concern for the welfare of others Demonstrates problem-solving attitude Demonstrates commitment to social improvement	Completes, describes, differentiates, explains, follows, forms, initiates, invites, joins, justifies, proposes, reads, reports, selects, shares, studies, works
Recognizes the need for balance between freedom and responsibility in a democracy Recognizes the role of systematic planning in solving problems Accepts responsibility for his or her own behavior Understands and accepts his or her own strengths and limitations Formulates life plan in harmony with his or her abilities, interests, and beliefs	Adheres, alters, arranges, combines, compares, completes, defends, explains, generalizes, identifies, integrates, modifies, orders, organizes, prepares, relates, synthesizes
Displays safety consciousness Demonstrates self-reliance working independently Practices cooperation in group activities Uses objective approach in problem solving Demonstrates industry, punctuality, and self-discipline Maintains good health habits	Acts, discriminates, displays, influences, listens, modifies, performs, practices, proposes, qualifies, questions, revises, serves, solves, uses, verifies

TABLE V. A Classification of Educational Objectives in the Psychomotor Domain
(Simpson, 1972)

Description of the Major Categories in the Psychomotor Domain

1. Perception. The first level is concerned with the use of the sense organs to obtain cues that guide motor activity. This category ranges from sensory stimulation (awareness of a stimulus), through cue selection (selecting task-relevant cues), to translation (relating cue perception to action in a performance).

2. Set. Set refers to readiness to take a particular type of action. This category includes mental set (mental readiness to act), physical set (physical readiness to act), and emotional set (willingness to act). Perception of cues serves as an important prerequisite for this level.

3. Guided Response. Guided response is concerned with the early stages in learning a complex skill. It includes imitation (repeating an act demonstrated by the instructor) and trial and error (using a multiple-response approach to identify an appropriate response). Adequacy of performance is judged by an instructor or by a suitable set of criteria.

4. Mechanism. Mechanism is concerned with performance acts where the learned responses have become habitual and the movements can be performed with some confidence and proficiency. Learning outcomes at this level are concerned with performance skills of various types, but the movement patterns are less complex than at the next higher level.

5. Complex Overt Response. Complex overt response is concerned with the skillful performance of motor acts that involve complex movement patterns. Proficiency is indicated by a quick, smooth, accurate performance, requiring a minimum of energy. This category includes resolution of uncertainty (performs without hesitation) and automatic performance (movements are made with ease and good muscle control). Learning outcomes at this level include highly coordinated motor activities.

6. Adaptation. Adaptation is concerned with skills that are so well developed that the individual can modify movement patterns to fit special requirements or to meet a problem situation.

7. Origination. Origination refers to the creating of new movement patterns to fit a particular situation or specific problem. Learning outcomes at this level emphasize creativity based upon highly developed skills.

TABLE VI. Examples of General Instructional Objectives and Clarifying Verbs for the Psychomotor Domain

Illustrative General Instructional Objectives	Illustrative Verbs for Stating Specific Learning Outcomes
Recognizes malfunction by sound of machine Relates taste of food to need for seasoning Relates music to a particular dance step	Chooses, describes, detects, differentiates, distinguishes, identifies, isolates, relates, selects, separates
Knows sequence of steps in varnishing wood Demonstrates proper bodily stance for batting a ball Shows desire to type efficiently	Begins, displays, explains, moves, proceeds, reacts, responds, shows, starts, volunteers
Performs a golf swing as demonstrated Applies first-aid bandage as demonstrated Determines best sequence for preparing a meal	Assembles, builds, calibrates, constructs, dismantles, displays, dissects, fastens, fixes, grinds, heats, manipulates, measures, mends, mixes, organizes, sketches, works
Writes smoothly and legibly Sets up laboratory equipment Operates a slide projector Demonstrates a simple dance step	(Same list as for Guided Response)
Operates a power saw skillfully Demonstrates correct form in swimming Demonstrates skill in driving an automobile Performs skillfully on the violin Repairs electronic equipment quickly and accurately	(Same list as for Guided Response)
Adjusts tennis play to counteract opponent's style Modifies swimming strokes to fit the roughness of the water	Adapts, alters, changes, rearranges, reorganizes, revises, varies
Creates a dance step Creates a musical composition Designs a new dress style	Arranges, combines, composes, constructs, designs, originates

Chapter 5

Lower-Level Cognitive Outcomes

The lowest-level cognitive learning outcomes pertaining to knowledge are the easiest to identify and define. Thus, first attempts at stating objectives tend to focus on the following two intended learning outcomes.

Knowledge of terms
Knowledge of facts

This is understandable. Various studies evaluating teachers' classroom tests have revealed that 80 percent, or more, of the test questions were concerned with recalling factual information. Apparently, without careful consideration given to the intended learning outcomes, teachers tend to focus on teaching and testing for facts. If it does not do anything else, the *Taxonomy of Educational Objectives* makes us aware of the vast array of possible instructional outcomes ranging from simple to complex. Here we shall focus on identifying and stating intended learning outcomes at the lower levels of the cognitive domain. In the following chapter, we shall consider higher-level thinking skills.

Knowledge, Comprehension, and Application

Most content areas and most levels of instruction include intended learning outcomes at the *knowledge, comprehension*, and *application* levels. In some cases these terms can be used directly in the statements of the general instructional objectives, as shown in Box 5.1. In others, the statements may need to be modified to fit the instruction more closely. There is no advantage in forcing statements of objectives to fit a certain set of categories. These categories should simply serve as a guide for identifying objectives that go beyond the simple recall of factual information.

BOX 5.1 SAMPLE GENERAL INSTRUCTIONAL OBJECTIVES

Examples of knowledge, comprehension, and application outcomes in various content areas.

Mathematics

   Knows the meaning of terms and symbols.
   Comprehends mathematics concepts and processes.
   Applies concepts and processes to mathematical problems.

Reading

   Knows word meanings.
   Comprehends the literal meaning of written material.
   Applies reading skills to textbook material.

Writing

   Knows the mechanics of writing.
   Comprehends grammatical rules of writing.
   Applies writing skills in laboratory reports.

Science

   Knows scientific terms.
   Comprehends scientific concepts and principles.
   Applies concepts and principles.

Social Studies

   Knows facts about social problems.
   Comprehends effects of social problems on society.
   Applies problem solving approach to social problems.

Adapting Statements to Levels of Instruction

In some cases the intended learning outcomes can be adapted to the level of instruction by means of the specific learning outcomes. For example, knowledge of basic concepts might vary from the lower primary level to upper secondary levels (high school and college) as follows:

1. Knows basic concepts (lower primary level).
   1.1 Selects picture indicating relative position (e.g., first, last).
   1.2 Selects picture indicating relative size (e.g., biggest, smallest).
   1.3 Selects picture indicating relative amount (e.g., most, least).
   1.4 Selects picture indicating relative distance (e.g., farthest, nearest).
2. Knows basic concepts (upper secondary levels).
   2.1 Describes the characteristics of the concept.
   2.2 Identifies an example of the concept.

2.3 Identifies symbols representing the concept.

2.4 Distinguishes between the concept and similar concepts.

In other cases, the same general instructional objective and list of specific learning outcomes may be used at more than one instructional level; the increased difficulty is derived from the increased difficulty of the content. Reading comprehension, for example, can be defined by a given set of specific outcomes that are applicable to more than one instructional level as follows:

1. Comprehends a reading passage.

1.1 Identifies the main thought of a passage.

1.2 Identifies details stated in a passage.

1.3 Identifies the order of events stated in a passage.

1.4 Identifies relationships between events in a passage.

1.5 States inferences about the contents of a passage.

These specific learning outcomes indicate what students can do when they read with comprehension, and the complexity of the reading material will determine their level of comprehension.

In still other instances, it may be desirable to state the general instructional objectives to fit the content more closely and to use the knowledge, comprehension, and application categories only as a general frame of reference. At the elementary level, and especially at the primary level where the learning outcomes are rather limited, more specific statements might better clarify instructional intent. For example, we might write general instructional objectives and lists of specific learning outcomes as follows:

1. Distinguishes among geometric shapes (Knowledge).

1.1 Draws a given shape (e.g., circle, square).

1.2 Selects an object representing a given shape (e.g., ball, box).

1.3 Identifies shapes of objects in a picture (e.g., building, lake).

1.4 Describes objects using the names of shapes.

2. Interprets graphs (Comprehension).

2.1 Identifies the value of a given position on a graph.

2.2 Identifies the relative values of two given positions on a graph.

2.3 Describes the trend indicated by a graph.

2.4 Distinguishes between statements that are supported and unsupported by a graph.

3. Translates from verbal to mathematical form (Comprehension).

3.1 Converts words to numerals.

3.2 Converts words to mathematical symbols.

3.3 Converts verbal statements to mathematical formulas.

3.4 Writes an equation that represents a word problem.

4. Writes a well-organized paragraph (Application).

    4.1 States a main idea.

    4.2 Relates sentences to the main idea.

    4.3 Uses complete sentences.

    4.4 Uses descriptive words to emphasize points.

    4.5 Arranges sentences in a meaningful sequence.

    4.6 Uses capitals and punctuation correctly.

    4.7 Spells words correctly throughout paragraph.

    4.8 Maintains correct grammatical usage throughout paragraph.

Even at higher levels of instruction, the outcome should, of course, be written in the manner that best describes the intended learning outcomes, and not be restricted to statements using the terms "knows," "comprehends," and "applies."

Adapting Statements to Areas of Instruction

In stating instructional objectives, we have attempted to keep the statements as free of particular course content as possible so that they can be used with various units of instruction. The statements of intended learning outcomes should indicate how students are to react, and the content in different instructional units will indicate what they are to react toward. Nevertheless, the nature of the course being taught will affect the types of learning outcomes to be identified and how they are to be stated. For example, two different instructional areas may state outcomes at the understanding level, but the specific learning outcomes describe different types of student performance to represent understanding as follows:

1. Understands biological principles.

    1.1 Identifies the principle in restated form.

    1.2 Identifies examples of the principle.

    1.3 States hypotheses that are in harmony with the principle.

    1.4 Distinguishes between correct and incorrect applications of the principle.

2. Understands modern drama.

    2.1 Identifies the main theme of a given play.

    2.2 Describes the dramatist's purpose in the play.

    2.3 Describes how character development was handled in the play.

    2.4 Explains how literary devices were used in the play.

    2.5 Describes how sub-plots contributed to the main theme of the play.

There are some areas of instruction where the knowledge, comprehension, application *hierarchy* does not fit well. It seems most appropriate for content areas, such as science and social studies, and less useful in courses emphasizing performance skills. A course like typing, for example, stresses primarily knowledge and skill outcomes; there is little value in attempting to force the outcomes into the comprehension and application categories. Typing is an application of skill, but this type of application is not the same as the "application" category in the *Taxonomy*. The latter refers to the use of principles to solve problems that are new to the students. Thus, it represents a higher level of understanding than comprehension, and does not refer to performance skills like typing.

There are a number of areas where knowledge and skill play a major role. For example, at the elementary level such areas as speaking, spelling, and simple computational skills would fall in this category. At the secondary level such courses as art, music, vocational courses, and physical education might place major emphasis on knowledge and skill. Stating outcomes in the skill area will be described in a later chapter. The main point here is, don't attempt to use the hierarchy of *knowledge, comprehension,* and *application* if it doesn't apply. In teaching how to play basketball, for example, don't use objectives like "Comprehends the rules of play" and "Applies the rules of play during a game." This implies a higher level of cognitive outcomes than the activity warrants. It is much better to state these outcomes as follows:

Knows the rules of play.

Follows the rules during a game.

Statements such as these indicate what the students are expected to be able to do, without implying there is some higher level of understanding involved. Of course, to clearly describe student performance each general objective would need to be defined by a list of specific learning outcomes as illustrated earlier.

The Problem of Limiting Objectives to the Cognitive Domain

Although we are focusing here on learning outcomes in the cognitive domain, it must be recognized that some objectives cannot be limited to the cognitive area. Many forms of performance (e.g., laboratory work, giving a speech, and operating a computer) include elements of all three types of outcomes—cognitive, affective, and psychomotor. In some cases it is possible to break the performance down into each type of outcome. Laboratory performance, for example, could be broken down into the following three statements.

Knows laboratory procedures (cognitive).

Demonstrates skill in laboratory work (psychomotor).

Demonstrates scientific attitude in interpreting results (affective).

With statements such as these, we can evaluate laboratory work by focusing separately on each of the three categories. The students' knowledge of procedures can be evaluated by both testing and observation, the demonstration of skill by a rating of performance, and the scientific attitude by both observation and examination of the laboratory reports. Thus, such a break down enables us to isolate the cognitive element for evaluation purpose even though it might not be isolated during the instruction.

In other instances, breaking an intended outcome down into separate categories might destroy the integrated nature of the performance. In giving a speech, for example, the content of the speech, the stage presence and gestures used, and the attitudes reflected in the content and delivery of the speech are all part of the effectiveness of the speech and must be evaluated as an integrated whole. Although judgments about the content, delivery, and attitudes can be made separately after the speech has been given, they cannot be made apart from any particular speech. In these cases, the intended outcomes should be stated in such a way that they reflect the integrated nature of the activity. They should not be broken down into artificial categories just so the statements can be classified as cognitive, psychomotor, or affective. As noted earlier, use the *Taxonomy* categories as a guide but don't become a slave to this, or any other, classification system.

Summary

In preparing a set of instructional objectives, it is usually desirable to start with lower-level cognitive outcomes. These are easiest to identify and state, are applicable to many areas of learning, and are familiar to teachers at various levels of instruction. They are also helpful in getting teachers to move from simple knowledge outcomes to more complex learning outcomes.

Lower-level cognitive outcomes encompass instructional objectives that emphasize knowledge, comprehension, and application. This hierarchy provides a simple set of categories that can aid in writing instructional objectives that go beyond the recall of factual information. In getting started, however, it is helpful to keep in mind the following points.

1. The terms knowledge, comprehension, and application can be used directly in the statements of general instructional objectives, if they are appropriate to the instruction and can be defined by a list of specific learning outcomes that clarifies what is meant by knowing, comprehending, and applying.

2. Some general instructional objectives (e.g., Knows basic concepts) might be used at different levels of instruction if they are defined by an appropriate set of specific learning outcomes at each level.

3. In some cases, the same general objective and the same set of specific learning outcomes may be appropriate for different levels of instruction (e.g., Reading comprehension), and the increased difficulty of performance is derived from the increased complexity of the content at higher levels.

4. In some instances, the intended learning outcomes can be more clearly stated by using terminology that is more specific and more directly relevant to the instructional area than the simple know, comprehend, apply sequence. This is especially true of the primary level and of such courses as art, music, vocational, business, and physical education.

5. Avoid stating objectives at the comprehension and application levels, if the intended learning outcomes are concerned only with knowledge and performance skills (e.g., typing).

6. If an intended learning outcome is most clearly stated by including more than one type of outcome (i.e., cognitive, psychomotor, and affective), as in giving a speech, don't modify it simply so that it can be classified into separate categories. After all, your main task is to clarify your instructional intent—not to classify the objectives.

To repeat, once again, use the *Taxonomy* only as a guide—not a master. The knowledge, comprehension, application hierarchy provides a good frame of reference for getting started at this level, but within this framework the general instructional objectives and specific learning outcomes can be stated in many different ways.

Chapter 6

Higher-Level Thinking Skills

Attempting to identify and define intended learning outcomes that represent higher-level thinking skills is frequently confusing because thinking skills are classified in so many different ways. In the literature the terms critical thinking, creative thinking, and problem solving are commonly used as frameworks encompassing sets of thinking skills and strategies. The *Taxonomy of Educational Objectives* classifies all outcomes beyond the knowledge category as "intellectual abilities and skills" that can be used in understanding new situations and solving new problems.

Thinking strategies in problem solving typically include a sequence of activities such as (1) identifying and analyzing a problem, (2) applying past learning, (3) gathering new information, (4) organizing and comparing data, (5) analyzing elements and relationships, (6) clarifying and judging alternatives, and (7) summarizing a solution or selecting a course of action. Within this problem-solving process a number of specific thinking skills (e.g., identifies the adequacy of data) and affective behaviors (e.g., objectivity) are involved, as well as lower-level cognitive outcomes (e.g., knowledge of concepts) and general problem solving strategies (e.g., observing, asking questions).[1]

In this chapter the focus is on the thinking skills at the levels of analysis, synthesis, and evaluation in the *Taxonomy*. Rather than present a sequenced set of skills that may fit one problem and not others, or may vary from one content area to another, it was decided to present a collection of specific types of learning outcomes to use in writing instructional objectives at this level. In some cases the specific skill outcomes may be taught and tested separately (e.g., distinguishes between fact and opinion) because they enter into so many aspects of learning. More commonly, the skills will be taught and tested in relation to particular problems or situations in a specific content area.

The collection of specific types of learning outcomes presented in Box 6.1 makes it possible to select those outcomes that are most commonly used in a particular area. For example, *analysis* in science, social studies, English, mathematics, art, music, and

---

[1] For a more comprehensive and detailed description of a framework for thinking, see Robert J. Marzano, et al., *Dimensions of Thinking: A Framework for Curriculum and Instruction*, Association for Supervision and Curriculum Development, Alexandria, Virginia, 1988.

BOX 6.1 EXAMPLES OF SPECIFIC OUTCOMES INVOLVED IN THINKING SKILLS

ANALYSIS

Identifies—

adequacy	contradictions	inconsistencies	reasoning
assumptions	criteria	inferences	relationships
attributes	defects	limitations	relevance
bias	distortions	main ideas	stereotypes
causes	effects	nature of evidence	superstition
central issues	elements	organization	trends
completeness	errors	plausibility	validity
concepts	exceptions	problems	variables
consequences	fallacies	procedures	

Distinguishes between—

accurate and inaccurate	facts and value statements
cause and effect	plausible and implausible
consistent and inconsistent	possible and probable
dominant and subordinate	relevant and irrelevant
essential and unessential	summaries and conclusions
facts and conclusions	supportive and contradictory
facts and hypothesis	valid and invalid
facts and inferences	verifiable and unverifiable
facts and opinions	warranted and unwarranted

Infers—

assumptions	characteristics	motives	purposes
attitudes	conditions	organization	qualities
biases	moods	points of view	relationships

SYNTHESIS

Formulates—

classification systems	generalizations	principles
concepts	hypotheses	problems
conclusions	musical compositions	questions
designs	plans	stories
equations	poetry	summaries
explanations	predictions	theories

EVALUATION

Generates—

criteria	standards	procedures

Judges—

accuracy	correctness	significance
adequacy	credibility	standards
appropriateness	organization	usefulness
clarity	reasonableness	validity
cohesiveness	reasoning	values
completeness	relationships	worth
consistency	reliability	

vocational courses are likely to emphasize different specific outcomes because of the nature of the content or the types of problems to be solved. Similar differences will be found at the *synthesis* and *evaluation* levels. In addition, some problems or situations may involve relatively few specific skills while others require a comprehensive list. Thus, the collection of specific outcomes in Box 6.1 provides flexibility for selecting those that are most appropriate for particular situations in various content areas and at various levels of instruction. The lists, of course, are not exhaustive but merely suggestive of the many specific skills involved in thinking.

In confining our lists of specific outcomes to higher-level thinking skills at the analysis, synthesis, and evaluation levels, the following types of outcomes important to problem solving are not being considered here.

1. Lower-level cognitive outcomes (knowledge, comprehension, application). These play an important role in the total thinking process but were covered in the last chapter.
2. General thinking strategies such as asking questions, observing, comparing, and organizing data.
3. Affective outcomes such as attitudes, curiosity, independent thought, honesty, objectivity, open mindedness, perseverance, respect for evidence, and willingness to suspend judgment. Affective outcomes are an integral part of thinking but will be described in the next chapter.

In some cases it may be necessary to incorporate into a description of an objective involving thinking-skill outcomes some elements of lower-level outcomes (e.g., interpretation), general thinking strategies (e.g., asks questions), or affective outcomes (e.g., curiosity). There is no attempt here to isolate them except as a basis for discussion and illustration.

Making a Content-Free List of Outcomes

Stating outcomes that are relatively content free may be useful where the same outcomes are to be used with different units or areas of instruction. The following lists, for example, will indicate how students are to perform when they demonstrate thinking skills in reading, evaluating an argument, or planning an experiment. The statements are general enough to be used with various types of reading material and course content.

1. Demonstrates thinking skills in reading.
    1.1 Distinguishes between main ideas and supporting details.
    1.2 Distinguishes between facts and opinions.
    1.3 Distinguishes between facts and inferences.
    1.4 Identifies cause–effect relations.
    1.5 Identifies errors in reasoning.
    1.6 Distinguishes between valid and invalid conclusions.
    1.7 Identifies assumptions underlying conclusions.
2. Evaluates arguments for and against a proposal.
    2.1 Identifies the accuracy of statements.
    2.2 Identifies bias in statements.
    2.3 Distinguishes between relevant and irrelevant statements.
    2.4 Distinguishes between supportive and nonsupportive statements.
    2.5 Identifies the assumptions underlying an argument.
    2.6 Identifies the adequacy of an argument.
    2.7 Identifies the consistency of the facts supporting an argument.
    2.8 Identifies the credibility of sources cited in an argument.
3. Prepares a plan for an experiment.
    3.1 Identifies the problem to be solved.
    3.2 Formulates questions relevant to the problem.
    3.3 Formulates hypotheses in appropriate verbal or mathematical form.
    3.4 Selects controls for variables.
    3.5 Formulates experimental procedures.
    3.6 Formulates observation and measurement procedures.
    3.7 Describes the methods of data analysis.
    3.8 Describes how the results will be presented.

Other specific outcomes could be stated for these general objectives to make them more comprehensive and detailed, or to adapt them to a particular type of reading, experiment, or proposal. These lists, however, indicate the approximate amount of detail needed for clarifying what students can do when they have achieved these higher-level cognitive outcomes.

Adapting Statements to Levels of Instruction

As with lower-level cognitive outcomes, higher-level thinking objectives can be adapted to the various levels of instruction by (1) modifying the lists of specific learning outcomes, (2) varying the difficulty of the problem to be solved or the content to be evaluated, or (3) modifying both the general objective and the specific learning outcomes.

Instruction at the elementary level typically uses fewer and more simply stated specific learning outcomes to define an instructional objective. Thus, if we were to define the instructional objective in reading, illustrated earlier, we might prepare a list such as the following:

1. Demonstrates thinking skills in reading.

    1.1 Identifies the main ideas in a story.

    1.2 Distinguishes between stated details and implied information.

    1.3 Describes the sequence of events in the story.

    1.4 Tells why particular events happened in the story.

    1.5 Describes why the characters acted as they did.

    1.6 Summarizes the meaning of the story.

An example of using the same objective and list of specific learning outcomes at different levels of instruction and varying the difficulty by selecting problems or content at different levels of difficulty can be easily accomplished with the earlier objective "Evaluates arguments for and against a proposal." Relatively simple proposals can be selected for use at lower levels of instruction and more complex proposals regarding social, economic, or political issues can be used at higher levels. Although the specific learning outcomes may need to be varied slightly to fit different instructional levels or issues, the specific learning outcomes listed earlier for this objective are widely adaptable.

With some modification and simplification of the specific learning outcomes listed for the objective "Prepares a plan for an experiment," it would be possible to use the objective at the elementary level. In some cases, however, it would be desirable to modify the general objective to indicate an experiment for a particular problem and to list the specific outcomes in terms of that problem as follows:

1. Designs an experiment to prove that a plant grows better in some soils than others.

    1.1 Predicts the type of soil in which plants grow best.

    1.2 Describes each type of soil to be used.

    1.3 Describes the factors to be considered in plant selection.

    1.4 Lists the factors to be kept constant.

    1.5 Describes the measurement procedures to be used.

    1.6 Describes the procedural steps and length of the experiment.

    1.7 Describes how the results will be presented.

Stating the objective and specific learning outcomes as specific as this does not permit their use with other problems, although the general pattern of specific statements does provide a framework that can serve as a guide. Also, in stating the experimental problem as part of the objective, the students, of course, are not given practice in problem identification. Finally, in simplifying the statements care must be taken not to reduce the student performance from a higher-level thinking skill to a lower-level routine activity.

Adapting Statements to Areas of Instruction

Discussions of critical thinking, creative thinking, problem solving, and other higher-level thinking skills commonly list the operations or skills independent of a particular area of content, somewhat as we have done in Box 6.1. Some types of performance are more appropriate to one area of content than others, however, and this typically can be shown in the selection of specific learning outcomes used to describe the general objective as follows:

1. Demonstrates ability to solve problems (Social Studies).
    1.1 Identifies the main idea in the problem.
    1.2 States the problem in question form.
    1.3 Selects relevant source materials.
    1.4 Analyzes source materials to obtain answers to the problem.
    1.5 Distinguishes between noncausal relations and cause–effect relations.
    1.6 Summarizes the findings from the source material.
    1.7 States conclusions that answer the problem question.
2. Demonstrates ability to solve problems (Mathematics).
    2.1 Analyzes a word problem.
    2.2 Identifies the information relevant to solving the problem.
    2.3 Translates words into numerals and symbols.
    2.4 Formulates an equation that represents the problem.
    2.5 Estimates the approximate answer to the problem.
    2.6 Solves the equation to answer the problem.
    2.7 Verifies the problem answer using an alternate method.

The intended learning outcomes may, of course, also be more closely adapted to a particular area of instruction by also modifying the general instructional objective. Here we are simply showing how a common instructional objective can be adapted by altering the types of student performance that represent the "ability to solve problems."

Summary

Higher-level thinking skills are commonly discussed in the literature under such headings as critical thinking, creative thinking, and problem solving. These are simply frameworks encompassing a collection of thinking skills and strategies. Because of the increased emphasis on thinking skills, the processes and skills are being redefined in different ways. The various frameworks best serve as a pool of types of student performance from which to select when preparing instructional objectives at this level. We have used the *Taxonomy* levels of analysis, synthesis, and evaluation to form such a pool. It includes a collection of the most widely used specific outcomes associated with higher-level thinking skills in the cognitive area.

When preparing instructional objectives in this area, it is important to keep in mind the following points.

1. The statements should take into account that the problems or situations must be new to the students. Without this novelty, the outcomes cannot be regarded as representative of thinking skills.

2. In stating and defining instructional objectives, use only the skill outcomes that are relevant to your level and area of instruction. Avoid describing thinking as a fixed set of skills and strategies.

3. Wherever possible, keep your objectives and specific skill outcomes relatively content free so that they can be used with different units of study.

4. Some general instructional objectives can be used at different levels of instruction by modifying the lists of specific skill outcomes, or by varying the difficulty of the problems to be solved.

5. Some general instructional objectives can be adapted to different areas of instruction by modifying the lists of specific skills. In other cases it is best to modify both the general instructional objective and the list of specific skills to obtain greater relevance.

Although affective outcomes associated with thinking have not been discussed here because they will be considered in the following chapter, don't neglect the attitudes and other behaviors that play a vital role in effective thinking when preparing your complete list of outcomes.

Chapter 7

Affective Outcomes

Preparing intended learning outcomes in the affective area is more difficult than in the cognitive area for a number of reasons. First, there is the vagueness of the terminology used in this area. Affective outcomes are concerned with feelings and emotions that are described by an individual's dispositions, willingness, preferences, enjoyments, and similar terms that have a wide range of meanings and are difficult to describe in performance terms. Second, although some of the intended outcomes can be stated overtly (e.g., asks questions) others are covert and can only be inferred (e.g., feels confident). In the latter case, all we can do is state the types of behavior that best support the presence of the inferred characteristic. Third, affective outcomes are described in so many different ways. In the literature they are typically classified under such headings as attitudes, interests, appreciations, and adjustments. The affective domain of the *Taxonomy* is structured to cut across these categories and to describe behavior within them, ranging from simple responses to complex behavior patterns. An "interest" response, for example, may vary from a person being simply aware that an activity exists to a strong preference for engaging in it. Fourth, as affective behaviors move from simple to complex, as in the *Taxonomy*, they become increasingly internalized and integrated with other behaviors (both affective and cognitive) to form complex value systems and behavior patterns. Thus, at higher levels it is more difficult to isolate and state intended learning outcomes in specific terms without destroying their integrated nature. Also, at higher levels overt responses are less dependable as evidence of internal states. For example, individuals may feel insecure but act as though they were completely confident.

Basing Statements on the Taxonomy Categories

One way to start in this area is to review the categories in the affective domain of the *Taxonomy* and use these categories as a guide. Using this procedure might result in statements such as the following:

1. Participates in classroom activities (Receiving and Responding).
    1.1 Listens attentively.
    1.2 Asks relevant questions.
    1.3 Participates in classroom discussion.
    1.4 Volunteers for special tasks.
    1.5 Contributes material for the bulletin board.
    1.6 Helps others when requested.
2. Shows concern for the welfare of others (Valuing).
    2.1 Asks others if they need help.
    2.2 Helps others with their problems.
    2.3 Shares materials with others.
    2.4 Encourages others to do well.
    2.5 Meets obligations in doing group work.
    2.6 Assists those reluctant to participate in group work.
    2.7 Obtains permission before using others' materials.
    2.8 Thanks and commends others, when appropriate.
3. Formulates a rationale concerning the role of society in conserving natural resources (Organization).
    3.1 Relates the needs of society to the conservation of resources.
    3.2 Describes the probable effects on society if resources are wantonly used.
    3.3 Describes the probable effects on society if the use of resources is overly restricted.
    3.4 States personal position reflecting a reasonable balance between the needs of society and the needs to conserve resources.
4. Respects the scientific process (Characterization).
    4.1 Favors evidence that results from scientific studies.
    4.2 Seeks objectivity in the interpretation of evidence.
    4.3 Changes opinions when evidence is contrary to beliefs.
    4.4 Suspends judgment when evidence is inadequate.
    4.5 Shows skepticism when statements are unsupported.
    4.6 Questions evidence derived from inadequate studies.
    4.7 Bases ideas and opinions on the best scientific evidence available.

These examples illustrate some of the difficulties mentioned earlier in stating affective outcomes. At the lower levels, the specific learning outcomes can be more easily stated in terms of overt behavior that can be observed by the teacher. At the higher levels where the desired behavior becomes more internalized and integrated, the descriptive terminology becomes more vague and refers to feelings and attitudes. This typically requires assessment by means of self-report methods and other techniques for getting at an individual's internal state.

Basing Statements on Traditional Categories

Because affective outcomes are typically described in the literature under the categories of attitudes, interests, appreciations, and adjustments, some teachers prefer to state objectives using these frameworks. When this is done, the *Taxonomy* can still be useful by helping in the statement of specific learning outcomes. With our two-step method of defining intended learning outcomes, a general instructional objective (e.g., Interest in reading) may be useful at different levels of instruction, but the specific learning outcomes clarify the types of performance expected at a particular level. Thus, the *Taxonomy* can assist in stating the specific outcomes at the appropriate performance level.

Attitudes are probably the most common affective outcome stressed by teachers. Although the major emphasis in teaching may be on cognitive outcomes or skill learning, most teachers would want their students to develop a favorable attitude toward their area of instruction and toward learning in general. In addition, other attitude outcomes may constitute an important component of the course. In science courses, for example, the development of a scientific attitude is typically a major objective of the instruction. The following example illustrates how this objective might be defined by a list of specific learning outcomes.

1. Displays a scientific attitude.

    1.1 Demonstrates curiosity in identifying problems.

    1.2 Seeks natural causes of events.

    1.3 Demonstrates openmindness when seeking answers.

    1.4 Suspends judgment until all evidence is available.

    1.5 Respects evidence from credible sources.

    1.6 Shows objectivity in analyzing evidence and drawing conclusions.

    1.7 Shows willingness to revise conclusions as new evidence becomes available.

The following statements of intended learning outcomes illustrate how objectives might be written for other traditional categories found in the literature.

2. Demonstrates interest in mathematics.

    2.1 Asks questions that indicate curiosity about math.

    2.2 Asks for extra problems to solve.

    2.3 Completes assignments on time.

    2.4 Brings examples of math problems to class.

    2.5 Helps others with math problems.

    2.6 Seeks ways to improve math learning.

    2.7 Uses math in out of school activities.

    2.8 Asks about careers in math.

3. Appreciates good literature.

    3.1 Describes the differences between good and poor literature.

    3.2 Distinguishes between selections of good and poor literature.

3.3 States reasons for classifying a selection as good or poor.

3.4 Selects and reads good literature during free-reading period.

3.5 Explains why he/she likes the selections that are read.

3.6 Describes his/her emotional reactions to the selections.

3.7 Expresses a desire for more time to read good literature.

4. Demonstrates good social adjustment.

4.1 Interacts harmoniously with others.

4.2 Shares ideas with others.

4.3 Confines classroom discussions to the issues.

4.4 Shows concern for the needs and feelings of others.

4.5 Is selected by others for group activities.

4.6 Cooperates with others in carrying out activities.

4.7 Is trustworthy in dealing with others.

4.8 Is courteous and considerate in working with others.

There are, of course, many other types of objectives that could be listed here. All we are attempting to do is illustrate the various ways that objectives might be stated and defined in the affective area.

In some cases it might be necessary to consider the types of assessment to be made when writing objectives. If observations are to be the main method of evaluating the intended outcomes (e.g., using rating scales or checklists), then it will be necessary to attempt to state the specific outcomes in terms of overt behavior only. If self-report instruments are to be used (e.g., attitude scales and interest inventories), then the statements can include more emphasis on feelings, opinions, preferences, and other internal states. For some types of outcomes both methods of assessment may be appropriate.

Affective Outcomes and Thinking Skills

Thinking involves both cognitive and affective components. In the last chapter we described and illustrated thinking-skill outcomes in the cognitive area. Here we shall focus on the affective aspects of thinking. Although they are separated for discussion purposes, they are, of course, integrated in various ways in practice.

A collection of some of the more common types of specific affective behaviors associated with thinking skills are shown in Box 7.1. These lists make it possible to select affective behaviors that are most appropriate for a particular situation. In some cases they might be included as part of a separate objective concerned with attitudes, as in our earlier illustration "Displays a scientific attitude." In other cases they might be included along with cognitive components in describing the application of thinking skills to some content area or some type of problem solving. As with the cognitive components of thinking, a particular objective may include relatively few affective behaviors or a large number, depending on the nature of the objective and the level of instruction.

BOX 7.1 EXAMPLES OF SPECIFIC AFFECTIVE BEHAVIORS IN THINKING

Demonstrates—

care in observing	originality
curiosity	perseverance
independent thought	respect for evidence
integrity	willingness to suspend judgment
objectivity	willingness to revise opinions
openmindedness	

Disposition to seek—

alternative answers	natural causes
confirming data	reasons for events
contrary points of view	relevant information
credible sources	verifiable facts

Appreciates importance of—

a clearly stated problem	social consequences of findings
care in observation	persistence
commitment to the task	preciseness of results
extending effort	questioning of results
orderly procedures	verification of results
sampling effect on findings	viewpoints of others

In defining the application of thinking skills to the solution of problems, the cognitive components and affective components can become closely integrated, resulting in a list of specific outcomes as follows:

1. Applies thinking skills in solving social problems.

    1.1 Identifies a common social problem.

    1.2 Analyzes the problem and related issues.

    1.3 States the problem and issues clearly.

    1.4 Gathers relevant information from credible sources.

    1.5 Distinguishes between facts and opinions.

    1.6 Identifies bias and other distortions in statements.

    1.7 Seeks viewpoints of others on the problem.

    1.8 Suspends judgment until information is complete.

    1.9 Identifies factors causing and contributing to the problem.

    1.10 Describes possible solutions to the problem.

    1.11 Describes the need for social action.

Note that although an attempt was made to define this objective in performance terms, affective elements pervade the statements. We can infer from the statements, for example, that the importance of a clearly stated problem is recognized (1.3), that there is a disposition to seek relevant information and use credible sources (1.4), that objectivity is being sought (1.5 and 1.6), that the viewpoints of others (1.7) and suspending judgment (1.8) is considered important, and that there is a disposition to seek causes (1.9) before obtaining solutions to a problem. Our inferences concerning these affective outcomes will, of course, require more than this one sample of behavior before they can be accepted as evidence of consistent tendencies or dispositions. All we are attempting to do here is to illustrate how affective outcomes might be included when defining thinking skills in problem solving.

Summary

Writing objectives in the affective area is much more difficult than in the cognitive area, and we typically must be satisfied with statements that are less precise than we would like. The difficulty is due to the fact that (1) the terminology used to describe affective behavior is vague, (2) some of the outcomes are covert (e.g., feelings) and can only be inferred, (3) the outcomes are classified in so many different ways, and (4) as affective behaviors move from simple to complex they become increasingly internalized and integrated with other behaviors, making it difficult to isolate and state them in specific terms.

Affective outcomes can be stated in terms of the *Taxonomy* categories, or the traditional categories found in the literature (e.g., attitudes, interests, appreciations, and adjustments). In the latter case, the *Taxonomy* still might be helpful in stating the specific outcomes at the appropriate performance level.

Affective outcomes play an important role in thinking and at higher levels become integrated with the cognitive component. The specific affective behaviors relevant to thinking can best be viewed as a collection of specific outcomes from which to select those that are most appropriate for a particular situation. In some cases they might be stated separately to define an affective objective (e.g., scientific attitude), whereas in others they might be combined with cognitive outcomes to define the use of thinking skills in decision making or problem solving.

When preparing instructional objectives in this area, it is important to keep in mind the following points.

1. State the outcomes in terms of overt behavior whenever possible, but don't neglect inner feelings if they are an important element in the objective.
2. Use as precise terminology as you can in describing behavior, but don't neglect outcomes that are important but cannot be stated in precise terms.
3. When describing complex outcomes, it may be necessary to combine cognitive and affective outcomes in the same list of statements.
4. In some cases, it may be desirable to consider the form of assessment to be used when defining a general instructional objective, to help determine how to state the specific learning outcomes. For example, don't include statements describing inner feelings unless some type of self-report method is to be used.

Chapter 8

Performance Outcomes

Performance outcomes play an important role in the instructional program. At the primary level, speaking, singing, handwriting, drawing, and similar performance outcomes are basic to the instruction. At higher levels of instruction, performance outcomes include laboratory skills, communication skills, and various special performance skills in agriculture, art, business, home economics, industrial education, music, and physical education. Despite their significance as valued learning outcomes, they are frequently neglected when writing objectives and planning for the evaluation of student learning. This is due, at least in part, to the difficulty and time consuming nature of performance evaluation. It is much simpler to measure *knowledge about* an activity than to evaluate actual *performance of* the activity. The task of evaluating performance can be made easier, however, by clearly defining the elements involved in the performance.

Performance outcomes in the school vary from those that place major emphasis on motor skill (e.g., handwriting, swimming) to those that are highly integrated with cognitive and affective outcomes (e.g., performs an experiment). Although the psychomotor domain in Chapter 4 focuses more directly on motor skills, we shall be concerned with all types of performance outcomes in this chapter. Whenever a student must *do* something rather than *tell about it*, we are concerned with a performance outcome.

When preparing objectives in this area, it is possible to focus on (1) the procedures or process during the performance, (2) the product resulting from the performance, or (3) both the procedures and the product. In giving a speech, for example, it is the performance itself that is important. In writing a theme, however, it is the product that is the focus of attention. The procedures can vary considerably in producing a high quality theme. However, in some areas, such as typing, emphasis is given to both the procedures (e.g., use of the touch system) and the product (e.g., well-typed letter). We shall describe and illustrate how to write objectives in each of the three areas.

Writing Objectives for Procedure Outcomes

In stating and defining performance objectives, the focus should be on the performance itself (e.g., the process) when:

58

1. The act of performing is the main outcome, or there is no product.
2. A diagnosis of the performance is needed to improve learning.
3. The performance is based on a collection of elements or series of steps that can be identified.

For any particular performance there are a number of elements, or procedures, that are crucial to a successful performance. Thus, in writing objectives in this area it is necessary to analyze the performance to identify those elements or procedural steps that define a satisfactory performance. These are then listed as specific learning outcomes under the general objective as follows:

1. Presents an oral report to the class.
    1.1 States the topic at the beginning of the report.
    1.2 Speaks clearly and loud enough to be heard.
    1.3 Uses language appropriate for the report.
    1.4 Uses correct grammar.
    1.5 Speaks at a satisfactory rate.
    1.6 Looks at the class members when speaking.
    1.7 Uses natural movements and appears relaxed.
    1.8 Presents the material in an organized manner.
    1.9 Holds the interest of the class.
2. Uses laboratory equipment properly (Science).
    2.1 Selects appropriate equipment for an experiment.
    2.2 Assembles equipment correctly for the experiment.
    2.3 Manipulates equipment as needed during the experiment.
    2.4 Measures accurately with proper measuring device.
    2.5 Follows safety rules in conducting experiment.
    2.6 Uses materials without wasting any.
    2.7 Completes experiment within time limits.
    2.8 Cleans equipment and returns to proper place.
3. Applies varnish correctly.
    3.1 Sands and prepares surface properly.
    3.2 Wipes dust from surface with appropriate cloth.
    3.3 Selects appropriate brush.
    3.4 Selects varnish and checks varnish flow.
    3.5 Pours needed amount of varnish into clean container.
    3.6 Puts brush properly into varnish (one-third of bristle length).
    3.7 Wipes excess varnish from brush on inside edge of container.
    3.8 Applies varnish to surface with smooth strokes.
    3.9 Works from center of surface toward the edges.

3.10 Brushes with the grain of the wood.

3.11 Uses light strokes to smooth the varnish.

3.12 Checks surface for completeness.

3.13 Cleans brush with appropriate cleaner.

3.14 Does *not* pour excess varnish back into can.

3.15 Cleans work area.

In reviewing these objectives, note that in some cases the order of the specific learning outcomes is not especially important (e.g., oral report), whereas in others they define a systematic, step-by-step procedure (e.g., the application of varnish). Where order of procedure is significant in the performance, care should be taken to place the outcomes in the proper order. This will make it easier to judge the performance and to detect errors.

When specific learning outcomes are properly stated, they can be easily converted to a checklist by simply adding a place to check "yes" or "no" for each procedure, or to a rating scale by adding a place to rate each procedure as it is performed. These instruments can be used to both guide student learning and to evaluate their performance. Thus, when writing the list of specific learning outcomes, use language that is easily understood by students and that will provide clear statements for checking or rating learning progress.

Writing Objectives for Product Outcomes

Performance objectives should focus on the product resulting from the performance when:

1. The product is the main outcome of the performance.
2. The product has identifiable characteristics that can be used in evaluating the quality of the product.
3. There is considerable variation in the procedures that can be used in producing the product, or the procedures are not observable to the instructor (e.g., out-of-class work).

If the objective indicates a product and the characteristics of the product can be identified and clearly defined, the specific learning outcomes are stated as criteria that describe a high-quality product as follows:

1. Constructs a bar graph.

1.1 Uses a separate bar for each measure.

1.2 Matches length of each bar to data.

1.3 Arranges bars in some logical order.

1.4 Makes bars wider than spaces between them.

1.5 Uses scale and guide lines that make bars easy to interpret.

1.6 Identifies each bar with a label.

1.7 Uses title that clearly indicates the nature of the graph.

2. Writes an effective composition.

    2.1 Expresses ideas clearly.

    2.2 Uses ideas that are logical.

    2.3 Relates ideas to the main thesis.

    2.4 Organizes the thesis to fit the topic.

    2.5 Writes well-structured, relevant paragraphs.

    2.6 Uses parts of speech correctly.

    2.7 Uses words that effectively convey meaning.

    2.8 Spells all words correctly.

    2.9 Uses correct punctuation.

As with procedure outcomes, the list of specific statements defining a product can be easily converted to a checklist or rating scale for use in performance assessment. Thus, keep the statements simple and clear so that the assessment instrument can be used by students, both as a guide to learning and as a basis for self evaluation.

In addition to the importance of products in general education, there are many specialized areas where a product is important. Courses in art, business, home economics, and industrial education include products that are highly valued as learning outcomes. In most of these areas, however, both the procedures and the product are to be included when defining performance objectives.

Focusing on Both Procedure and Product Outcomes

Performance objectives should include both procedure and product outcomes when:

1. There is a clear set of procedures for producing the product (e.g., cooking recipe, steps for constructing a woodworking project).

2. Learning is at an early stage and the product can be improved by correcting procedural errors.

3. Both the process and the product have identifiable elements that can be described and observed.

Most performance objectives in the school are concerned with entry level performance. The aim is to learn the proper procedures and to obtain a *satisfactory* level of performance, rather than a high degree of proficiency (unless it's a trade or professional school). Thus, wherever feasible, focus should be directed toward both the procedures used and the product. By adequately describing the procedures, we can provide guidelines for diagnosing and improving those elements of the performance that will result in a better product. Our description of the product provides a means for evaluating the effect of the improved procedures on the quality of the product and the level of proficiency attained.

A generalized set of specific outcomes for the procedures and product of a woodworking project might be stated as follows:

1. Follows proper procedures.

    1.1 Follows the steps listed in the project plan.

    1.2 Selects appropriate materials to use.

    1.3 Selects proper tools for project.

    1.4 Uses tools correctly for each task.

    1.5 Works carefully to avoid waste of materials.

    1.6 Uses time efficiently and completes project on schedule.

2. Constructs a quality product.

    2.1 Dimensions of product match specifications.

    2.2 Overall appearance reflects care in construction.

    2.3 Finish is even and of high quality.

    2.4 Joints are smooth and fit tightly.

    2.5 Parts (e.g., drawers) fit properly and function well.

These outcomes are stated generally enough that they would fit various woodworking projects. When stating outcomes for a particular project, they could, of course, be stated in more specific terms.

When both procedure outcomes and product outcomes are stated for the same performance objective, both can be included in the same checklist or rating scale. This provides a more comprehensive evaluation than either would alone and makes it possible to compare performance on the two dimensions.

Summary

Performance outcomes are an important type of learning in most areas of instruction but are frequently neglected when writing objectives and planning for the evaluation of student learning. This is partly due to the difficulty of evaluating performance. The task is considerably easier, however, if the performance objectives are clearly defined.

During the preparation of performance objectives, one can focus on (1) the procedure, (2) the product, or (3) both the procedure and the product. The focus depends on the nature of the objective. In some cases there is no product (e.g., speaking); in others, the product does not depend on a clearly defined set of procedures (e.g., writing a theme). Whenever both a procedure and a product are important and have identifiable elements, both procedure outcomes and product outcomes should be stated.

If performance objectives are clearly defined, the lists of specific outcomes for both procedures and products can be easily converted to checklists or rating scales for use in evaluating performance.

When preparing instructional objectives in this area, it is important to keep in mind the following points.

1. The procedures listed for a performance objective should include all those that are crucial to a successful performance.

2. If sequence is important, the procedures for a performance objective should be listed in proper order.

3. If the procedural steps are to be later converted to a checklist or rating scale, use language that is easily understood by students and that provides clear statements for checking or rating learning progress.

4. State product outcomes in terms of the characteristics that define a satisfactory product.

5. When both procedure outcomes and product outcomes are described for a performance objective, both should be included in the evaluation of performance.

Part III

Preparing and Using Instructional Objectives

Chapter 9

Preparing an Appropriate Set of Instructional Objectives

Now that you know how to state objectives so that they clearly convey the intended outcomes of instruction, let's take a look at the total process of preparing a list of objectives for a given course or instructional unit. How do you get started? What are some of the considerations? Where can you get ideas for objectives? How do you select and review objectives for the final list? In other words, how do you put it all together so that you end up with an appropriate list for the planned instruction?

Start with a Familiar Framework

One way to get started is to review the various types of outcomes shown in Box 9.1 and identify those areas that are relevant to your area of instruction. It is usually best to begin writing objectives in the categories of *knowledge*, *comprehension*, and *application*, because these are most familiar and the easiest to write. But don't stop there! Expand the list to include relevant objectives from the areas of thinking skills, affective outcomes, and performance outcomes. Some teachers prefer to obtain a list of general instructional objectives first and then to begin defining each one with a set of specific learning outcomes. During this process, it is not unusual to have to modify how some of the general objectives are stated.

When a fairly comprehensive list is obtained, a review of the cognitive, affective, and psychomotor domains of the *Taxonomy* (see Chapter 4) will help prevent any serious omissions in the final list. As noted in earlier chapters, don't feel compelled to match the categories in the *Taxonomy* but use it as a general guide to the vast array of learning outcomes that might be considered.

BOX 9.1 TYPES OF LEARNING OUTCOMES COMMON TO MANY AREAS AND LEVELS OF INSTRUCTION

Lower Level Cognitive Outcomes
    Knowledge of
    Comprehension of
    Application of

{
- Terms
- Facts
- Symbols
- Rules
- Concepts
- Principles
- Procedures

Higher Level Thinking Skills
    Analysis
    Synthesis
    Evaluation

{
- Identifying
- Distinguishing between
- Inferring
- Relating
- Formulating
- Generating
- Judging

Affective Outcomes
    Attitudes
    Interests
    Appreciations
    Adjustments

{
- Social
- Personal
- Scientific
- Educational
- Vocational
- Art, Music, Literature

Performance Outcomes
    Procedure
    Product
    Procedure and product

{
- Speaking
- Singing
- Drawing
- Computing
- Writing
- Laboratory skills
- Research skills
- Vocational skills
- Musical skills
- Physical skills

Getting Ideas for Instructional Objectives

In addition to the use of the *Taxonomy*, you can also get ideas when preparing instructional objectives by consulting lists of objectives developed by others and by reviewing your own teaching materials and methods.

1. Consulting Lists of Objectives Developed by Others. Reviewing lists of instructional objectives developed by others can also be useful in suggesting learning outcomes to consider and in noting the different ways objectives may be organized for a particular instructional area. Consulting other lists is usually most helpful after you have developed a tentative list of your own. At that point, you are less likely to uncritically adopt objectives that may be inappropriate for your instructional situation. Moreover, a review of other lists of objectives enables you to check the comprehensiveness of your list and to obtain ideas for improving it.

There are a number of sources for obtaining lists of instructional objectives. Most books on methods of teaching discuss objectives, present illustrative lists, and contain references that will help you locate others. The yearbooks and the special reports issued by the National Council of Teachers of English, the National Council of Teachers of Mathematics, the National Council for the Social Studies, and the National Science Teachers Association also contain suggested lists of objectives from time to time. In addition, books concerned with testing and evaluation in a particular instructional area will commonly devote some attention to instructional objectives.

An especially helpful guide for locating objectives in a specific instructional area is the *Encyclopedia of Educational Research*. It summarizes educational research on various topics, including research concerned with particular instructional areas. To use the *Encyclopedia of Educational Research*, simply consult the section on the teaching of the particular subject in which you are interested. There you will typically find references to statements of instructional objectives.

Another source of ideas for instructional objectives is found in the curriculum guides prepared on the state and local levels. Although some guides simply list the content to be covered at each grade level, others include lists of instructional objectives. Some college libraries keep files of such curriculum guides for teachers in training. Many of the larger schools may, on request, send you a copy of their curriculum guide. In obtaining ideas for instructional objectives from these various sources, you are likely to encounter two major problems. First, the lists of objectives in a given instructional area will show considerable variation in terms of emphasis and coverage. Thus, some lists will contain objectives that are not relevant to your situation, whereas others will neglect areas you consider important. Second, the lists will vary considerably in how the objectives are stated. Some will be stated in very general terms only, and others will be specified in great detail. Some will be stated in terms of the teacher, and others will be stated in terms of the student. Some will be stated as performance objectives, and others will be stated in nonperformance terms. This wide variation in content and form of statement simply means that care must be taken in adapting any list of objectives for your use. It also highlights the importance of developing a tentative list before consulting outside sources. If you have a reasonably clear idea of what the intended learning outcomes should be for your instructional area, you are less apt to be confused or undesirably influenced by the various lists of objectives. In the final analysis, your list of instructional objectives should, of course, be designed to fit your particular instructional situation.

2. Examining Your Own Teaching Materials and Methods. If you are presently teaching, your instructional procedures offer another source of ideas because instructional objectives are implicit in the materials and methods used in the classroom. Although the ideal situation would be to select teaching materials and teaching methods after identifying the expected learning outcomes, this procedure is not always possible. The textbook and other teaching materials may have been assigned by superiors. Likewise, your present teaching methods may have been determined partly by the required teaching materials and partly by past experience. In some cases, you may simply not have been exposed to this procedure for stating instructional objectives as learning outcomes until you had been teaching for some time. In any event, the materials and methods presently being used in your instruction provide another guide to the identification of instructional objectives. Your task is simply to make the implicit objectives explicit.

First, go through the subject matter included in your instruction, topic by topic, and ask yourself, "Why is this being taught?" Although the question may be difficult to answer at times, this procedure will help make explicit those objectives that are directly related to the nature of the subject matter.

Next, examine your other teaching materials in a similar manner. In using a world map, for instance, are you attempting to increase the students knowledge of specific facts, their understanding of geographic principles, their ability to interpret maps—or all three? Recalling how the map is used will help you identify the instructional objectives being sought.

Then examine your teaching methods. Some instructional objectives are direct outcomes of the methods used. Having students prepare written reports based on library work, for example, may imply that you value such outcomes as ability to locate information, ability to do independent work, and ability to write effectively. Similarly, having students participate in group activities may imply that you value outcomes concerned with interests, attitudes, or certain aspects of social adjustment.

In examining your present instructional procedures for implied objectives, you will most likely find some aspects of content and method that should be changed. This recognition of the need for change is a common byproduct of the examination process. When examined in the light of expected learning outcomes, some aspects of instruction appear hard to justify. If you are an English teacher who places high value on appreciation of poetry, for example, you might begin to question whether the students' memorization of poems is actually contributing to the attainment of this objective. Similarly, if you are a teacher of biology who requires students to spend endless hours drawing what they see through the microscope, you might begin to wonder if other procedures might not contribute more directly to their laboratory skills. Or if you are a social studies teacher, you might come to realize that additional work must be added to the course if critical thinking is to be developed. Whatever your instructional area, the process of reviewing your teaching methods and materials in order to identify the objectives implicit in their use is likely to have the desirable effect of bringing your instructional procedures and instructional objectives into closer alignment.

Considerations in Reviewing and Selecting Objectives

It is usually possible to identify many more objectives than can be achieved in a particular course or instructional unit. Thus, you must be selective when you compile the final list. The following questions will serve as criteria for appraising the adequacy of the objectives to be included.

1. Do the Objectives Indicate Learning Outcomes That Are Appropriate to the Instructional Area? This question has no simple answers, but it is one that has to be considered. Here we must turn to the recommendations of experts in the curriculum area in which you plan to teach. What learning outcomes do they consider to be most important? There will not be complete agreement here, but a review of their recommendations will help in identifying the objectives that have the greatest support of curriculum specialists. This review will prevent any serious omissions and will provide greater assurance that your final list of objectives is in harmony with the most recent developments in the area.

2. Do the Objectives Represent All Logical Learning Outcomes of the Instructional Area? Here we are concerned with the comprehensiveness and representativeness of the list of objectives. For example, are objectives included from all three areas of the *Taxonomy*—cognitive, affective, and psychomotor? Is there a proper balance among the three areas and within each area? There is a common tendency among teachers in areas where intellectual skills are dominant to overemphasize knowledge of specific facts and to neglect complex intellectual outcomes, attitudes, interests, and skills. On the other hand, teachers in areas where performance skills are dominant (art, music, physical education) frequently neglect the cognitive outcomes to be achieved. A more adequate balance of learning outcomes can be attained by reviewing the categories in the *Taxonomy of Educational Objectives* and by checking these categories against the recommendations of curriculum experts.

3. Are the Objectives Attainable by These Particular Students? To answer this question, we need to consider the ability of the students and their cultural background. Is the student group gifted, average, or of low ability? Or do we have a heterogeneous group, ranging from gifted to nearly mentally retarded? Are some or all of the students from culturally disadvantaged homes? The nature of the student group and their readiness for particular learning experiences are important considerations in formulating and selecting objectives. Closely related concerns are the time allowed for the instruction and the facilities and teaching materials available. The development of thinking skills and changes in attitude, for example, are extremely time-consuming because they depend on the cumulative effect of a long series of learning experiences. Similarly, some outcomes (e.g., skill in the scientific method) may require special laboratory facilities and special teaching materials. We are not suggesting here that otherwise desirable objectives be discarded, but simply that they may need to be modified to fit the student group and the instructional conditions under which they are to be achieved.

4. Are the Objectives in Harmony with the Philosophy of the School in Which the Instruction Is to Be Given? This would be an easy criterion to apply if each school had a clear statement of philosophy or a list of educational objectives to serve as a guide. Unfortunately, most schools do not. Thus, you must infer which outcomes are most valued in a particular school. If there appears to be an emphasis on independent work, self-discipline, freedom to explore new areas, and the democratic planning of activities, for example, these emphases should be reflected in the final list of instructional objectives. Similarly, if every teacher is expected to stress effective oral and written communication, thinking skills, and the relation of his or her subject to the other subjects in the school curriculum, a broader range of instructional objectives than might otherwise be the case will need to be included. In short, your instructional objectives should be in harmony with the stated or implicit objectives of the total school program.

5.   *Are the Objectives in Harmony with Basic Principles of Learning?* As we indicated earlier, our instructional objectives should be stated as desired learning outcomes. Thus, it is legitimate to ask to what extent our objectives are in harmony with what is known about the principles of learning. Some of the basic factors that should be considered are the following:

1. *Readiness.* Are the students mature enough to attain these particular objectives? Do the students have the necessary experiences and educational background to proceed successfully? Is there another level at which some of the objectives might be attained more readily?

2. *Motivation.* Do these particular objectives reflect the needs and interests of the students? Can they be restated or modified to be more closely related to the students' concerns? Is there another stage of development where these objectives would more closely fit the students' emerging interest?

3. *Retention.* Do these particular objectives reflect learning outcomes that tend to be retained longest (e.g., understanding, application, thinking skills)? Are there other objectives that might be more lasting and that should be included?

4. *Transfer value.* Do these particular objectives reflect learning outcomes that are widely applicable to new situations? Do the objectives include methods of study and modes of thinking that are most likely to contribute to future learning in the area?

These questions are not always easily answered, but they highlight the importance of considering the learning process when you formulate and select instructional objectives. Most general textbooks on educational psychology will provide extended discussions of the basic learning principles. It is sufficient to point out here that the more complex learning outcomes tend to be retained longer and to have greater transfer value. When they are appropriate to the developmental level of the learner, the more complex outcomes also have the greatest potential for arousing and maintaining student interest.

Preparing Instructional Objectives Cooperatively

It is desirable to have teachers prepare lists of instructional objectives cooperatively, wherever possible. This might involve teachers at the same grade level or in the same department working together, or it might involve committees of teachers representing all grade levels and all departments in the school. The cooperative development of objectives will ease the burden because the work can be divided up among the teachers. In addition, this procedure provides greater assurance that (1) teachers of the same course are emphasizing the same learning outcomes, (2) the sequence of instructional objectives from one grade level to the next or one course to the next is appropriate, (3) there is a minimum of overlap in single-course objectives (e.g., knowledge of facts), and (4) proper attention is given to multiple-course objectives (e.g., library skills) in each teacher's lists.

Because many schools are now using microcomputers to store objectives and relevant test items, it is even more important that instructional objectives be developed cooperatively. These pools of objectives and test items are likely to be more complete and useful when all teachers have participated in their preparation.

When a group of teachers is cooperatively preparing lists of instructional objectives, it may be desirable to provide descriptions of the types of student responses encompassed by commonly used action verbs. This will provide for standard usage of terms and greater uniformity in the statement of objectives. A sample test task may also be used to further clarify the type of student response expected. A simple format, such as that in Table VII, might be used.

Although the selected action verbs in Table VII are some of the more widely used verbs, there are, of course, many other verbs that might be used in stating specific learning outcomes. See Appendix B for a comprehensive list. From that collection, teachers might select those that are most relevant and define and illustrate them as shown in Table VII.

TABLE VII. Illustrations of How to Clarify Expected Student Responses for Selected Action Verbs[1]

Action Verb	Types of Response	Sample Test Task
Identify	Point to, touch, mark, encircle, match, pickup.	"Put an X under the right triangle."
Name	Supply verbal label (orally or in writing).	"What is this type of angle called?"
Distinguish between	Identify as separate or different by marking, separating into classes, or selecting out a common kind.	"Which of the following statements are *facts* (encircle F) and which are opinions (encircle O)?"
Define	Supply a verbal description (orally or in writing) that gives the precise meaning or essential qualities.	"Define each of the following terms."
Describe	Supply a verbal account (orally or in writing) that gives the essential categories, properties, and relationships.	"Describe a procedure for measuring relative humidity in the atmosphere."
Classify	Place into groups having common characteristics; assign to a particular category.	"Write the name of the type of pronoun used in each of the following sentences."
Order	List in order, place in sequence, arrange, rearrange.	"Arrange the following historical events in chronological order."
Construct	Draw, make, design, assemble, prepare, build.	"Draw a bar graph using the following data."
Demonstrate	Perform a set of procedures with, or without, a verbal explanation.	"Set up the laboratory equipment for this experiment."

[1] Reprinted from Gronlund, N. E., and Linn, R. L., *Measurement and Evaluation in Teaching*, 6th ed., New York: Macmillan, 1990. Used by permission.

Summary

The preparation of a list of instructional objectives for a particular course or instructional unit involves carefully selecting and defining those objectives that are most relevant to the instructional area. In getting started it is helpful to follow some type of systematic procedure, such as the following.

1. Review the various categories of cognitive, affective, and performance outcomes and attempt to identify a comprehensive list of general instructional objectives. Start with the knowledge, comprehension, and application categories and expand the list to include thinking skills, affective outcomes, and performance outcomes.

2. Consult lists of objectives developed by others, after you have a tentative list of your own, to obtain ideas for expanding and improving your list. If teaching, review your teaching materials and methods for ideas.

3. Define each general instructional objective with a list of specific learning outcomes, as described and illustrated in earlier chapters. A review of the *Taxonomy* domains in Chapter 4 may be helpful here in preventing any serious omissions in the final list.

4. Check your final list for appropriateness, representativeness, attainability, relationship to the total instructional program, and relationship to the basic principles of learning.

Chapter 10

Relating Objectives to Classroom Instruction

The final list of instructional objectives usually contains some learning outcomes that are considered essential for all students to achieve and others that allow for varying degrees of individual development. In arithmetic, for example, we might expect all students to know the multiplication table, but we anticipate considerable variation in the ability of students to solve problems requiring arithmetical reasoning. Similarly, we may consider it essential for all chemistry students to know the formulas of the chemical compounds studied, but we can expect wide variation in their ability to apply scientific principles to new situations. Learning outcomes that are considered *minimum essentials* are typically low-level outcomes that can be rather easily achieved by students and that serve as prerequisites to further learning in the area. Those outcomes at the *developmental level* represent goals toward which students may show different degrees of progress but which they never fully achieve. The ability to understand, to apply, to interpret, and to think, for example, typically depend on an extended period of development. Their complete attainment is not expected in any given course. All we can expect to do here is to define each objective in terms of those outcomes that are appropriate to the students' learning levels and that represent reasonable degrees of progress toward the objective.

Failure to distinguish between instructional objectives that are considered minimum essentials and those that encourage maximum development has caused considerable confusion in both teaching and testing. Some teachers tend to treat all objectives as minimum essentials and to strive for mastery on the part of all students. Where this is done, the more simple learning outcomes are stressed and teaching and testing tend to focus on specific learning tasks. In contrast to this approach, some teachers stress objectives at the developmental level only. They put so much emphasis on these more complex learning outcomes that they neglect the knowledge and skills that are prerequisite to a higher level of learning. To avoid these extremes, you should give consideration to both types of objectives when you prepare the list of intended learning outcomes, and you should use teaching and testing procedures that accommodate both types of outcomes.

Teaching and Testing at the "Minimum-Essentials Level"

The teaching emphasis at the *minimum-essentials level* is on shaping and modifying student behavior to fit a predetermined and clearly defined minimum level of performance. The learning outcomes are generally very specific and call for simple, independent responses. In fact, the objectives are frequently stated as tasks to be performed rather than as goals to work toward. Thus, we might have statements such as the following:

Adds single-digit whole numbers.

Identifies symbols used on weather maps.

Defines basic terms of unit.

Identifies parts of the microscope.

Such simple and clearly defined tasks make it possible to have a one-to-one relation between the stated objective, the teaching procedure, and the testing procedure. As illustrated in the following diagram, the specific learning outcome is stated, the specific task is directly taught, and the specific task is directly tested:

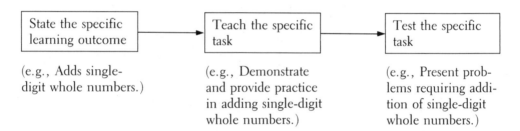

State the specific learning outcome	Teach the specific task	Test the specific task
(e.g., Adds single-digit whole numbers.)	(e.g., Demonstrate and provide practice in adding single-digit whole numbers.)	(e.g., Present problems requiring addition of single-digit whole numbers.)

This is the model used in programmed learning and in teaching at the training level. This model is very useful for illustrating the direct relationship between objectives, teaching, and testing in the learning of minimum essentials; that is, in those areas of learning where the desired outcome is to make all students perform alike at a specified *minimum* level. This model is inappropriate, however, for teaching and testing at the developmental level, as we shall see shortly.

Standards of performance are most frequently specified in the learning of minimum essentials. These standards may indicate that complete or nearly complete mastery is expected. Thus, a student may be expected "to identify *all* of the parts of a microscope," "to define 8 *out of* 10 terms," or "to solve 90 *percent* of the computational problems." Such standards are easily specified at this level because the learning outcomes are specific, independent, and easily defined.

Although stating the standards for a minimum level of performance is a simple process, determining what the standards should be is not. On what basis do you decide that a student should be able "to define 8 *out of* 10 terms"? Why shouldn't the student have to define 7, 9, or all 10? There is little evidence to support particular standards of achievement in the various subjects at different grade levels. Each teacher must depend on his or her own arbitrary judgment—based on the difficulty of the material, the nature of the student group, and the learning conditions that exist. Although such standards can provide rough guidelines for determining the extent to which a minimum level of performance is being achieved, you must always keep in mind that the standards are arbitrarily set and therefore highly tentative.

Teaching and Testing at the "Developmental Level"

The teaching emphasis at the *developmental level* is on encouraging each student to progress as far as possible toward predetermined goals. The instructional objectives here are typically more general than those at the mastery level. Rather than being stated as specific tasks to be performed, each objective represents a whole class of responses. Thus, the objectives provide direction for both the teacher and the student, without being overly restrictive with regard to the nature of the instruction or the types of learning activities to be engaged in by the student. They allow for an openness and exploration in the teaching–learning process that is absent in the closely prescribed shaping and molding process characteristic of the teaching of minimum essentials.

Because each instructional objective at the developmental level represents a large class of specific responses, all we can expect to do in defining each objective is to list a reasonably adequate *sample* of the specific learning outcomes. This process was described in Chapter 3 and is illustrated as follows:

1. Understands scientific principles.
    1.1 States the principle in his or her own words.
    1.2 Gives an example of the principle.
    1.3 Identifies predictions that are in harmony with the principle.
    1.4 Distinguishes between correct and incorrect applications of the principle.

The four specific learning outcomes listed under this objective help clarify what is meant by "Understands scientific principles," but these are just four of the numerous ways that *understanding* might be shown. Therefore, these four specific types of response are representative of the variety of responses that could describe the general objective. Because we are able to list only a sample of the types of performance we are interested in, these specific learning outcomes are not expected to be taught and tested on a one-to-one basis. In fact, were this method to be followed, learning would be of a rote nature, and responses could not be used as evidence of *understanding*. For example, if we were to teach a student to "state a principle in his or her own words" and later ask the student to "state the principle in his or her own words," the student's response would represent nothing more than the *recall* of previously learned material. The same would hold true for the other three specific learning outcomes. If all intended outcomes were taught in this manner, we would be functioning at a simple recall level, and the usefulness of the sample of performance as an indication of *understanding* would be destroyed. That is, the students would be able to demonstrate the types of performance included in the sample (in a rote manner) but would not be able to demonstrate the other types of performance also encompassed by the same instructional objective.

Teaching at the developmental level must be directed toward the general instructional objective and the total class of responses that it represents. The list of specific learning outcomes is mainly useful in providing an operational definition of the general objective and in providing guidelines for test construction.

The relation of teaching and testing to the objectives at the developmental level is illustrated as follows:

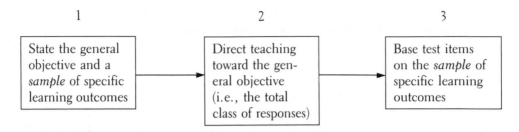

1	2	3
State the general objective and a *sample* of specific learning outcomes	Direct teaching toward the general objective (i.e., the total class of responses)	Base test items on the *sample* of specific learning outcomes

It will be noted in this diagram that the sample of specific learning outcomes that is identified in step 1 can also be used as a basis for developing the test items in step 3. In measuring such complex learning outcomes as understanding, however, the test items should go beyond what has been directly taught in step 2. In stating examples of a principle, for instance, the students should be required to state new examples (i.e., examples not discussed in class). Similarly, the application of principles should be concerned with new situations, and the interpretation of data should be based on data new to the students. It is only when the test items contain some novelty that we are able to go beyond the simple recall level of learning and to measure the more complex learning outcomes.

At the developmental level of learning where *maximum achievement* is the goal, useful standards of performance are extremely difficult, if not impossible, to define. Thus, it is usually necessary to describe test performance in relative terms; that is, in terms of where a given test score falls in some particular group. This may be a classroom group or, as in the case of standardized tests, a national group. In either instance, however, the test score indicates a relative level of achievement only; therefore, the nature of the group must be taken into account when you interpret the score.

A summary of some of the major differences between teaching and testing at the minimum-essentials level and at the developmental level is presented in Table VIII.

Using Objectives in Instructional Planning

The final list of objectives for a particular course or unit of work specifies the learning outcomes that are to result from the instruction. As we have noted, some of these outcomes will indicate a minimum level of performance required of all students, and some will indicate goals toward which varying degrees of progress can be expected. In any event, these objectives constitute the learning outcomes that are considered to have the greatest value for the students; therefore, they provide a sound basis for instructional planning. To be most effective, of course, the instructional objectives should be identified and defined before other instructional plans are made. When both the methods and materials of instruction and the procedures for evaluating student progress are selected in light of the intended learning outcomes, we can expect them to be more relevant and more effective.

One way to ensure that the instructional objectives, the teaching methods, and the evaluation techniques will be in harmony is to prepare a planning chart that includes all three. The two examples in Table IX, the first at the minimum-essentials level and

TABLE VIII. Summary Comparison of the Relation of Objectives to Teaching and Testing at Two Different Levels of Instruction

	Minimum-Essentials Level	Developmental Level
Teaching Emphasis	Shape and modify student behavior to fit a predetermined *minimum level of performance*.	Encourage and direct each student toward the *maximum level of development* he or she is capable of achieving.
Nature of the Objectives	Limited, specific, and completely defined tasks to be performed.	General objectives that provide direction and are defined by a *representative sample* of specific types of performance.
Relation of Teaching to the Objectives	Teaching is directed toward the specific task stated in the objective. Each *specific task* is taught on a one-to-one basis.	Teaching is directed toward the *general class of responses* that the objective represents, rather than toward the performance included in the particular sample.
Relation of Testing to the Objectives	Each specific task is tested directly on a one-to-one basis. Test items require students to demonstrate responses identical to those learned in class.	Only a *sample* of specific performance is tested for each objective. Test items require students to demonstrate previously learned responses in situations containing some novelty.
Specifying Performance Standards	Standards of minimum performance are easily specified, but they are usually set in an arbitrary manner.	Performance standards are difficult to specify. Achievement is typically reported in terms of *relative* position in some known group.

the second at the developmental level, illustrate the procedure for preparing a planning chart.

In using a planning chart, you must take care to prevent instruction from becoming subdivided into a series of separate teaching acts. The chart makes clear the relationship between the teaching methods, the evaluation techniques, and the desired learning outcomes, but you must not infer that each objective should be worked toward separately. "Knowledge of literary terms," for example, may receive direct attention early in the instruction, but this is a goal to work toward throughout the course. Similarly, when students work on the "Interpretation of literature," they would also give attention to specific facts concerning the literary work, to speaking and writing skills, to an appreciation of literature, and so on. In classroom instruction, we typically work on a number of different learning outcomes at the same time. What the chart does is to provide an overall plan to assure that each objective will receive the proper share of attention in the instructional process and that the methods of teaching and testing will be more relevant to the attainment of the desired learning outcomes. The chart, therefore, serves as a guide for our daily lesson planning. In these daily lesson plans, we can provide for the desired integration of the learning experiences and for their placement in proper sequence.

TABLE IX. Instructional Planning Chart

Instructional Objectives	Teaching Methods	Evaluation Techniques
Knows literary terms 1. Writes textbook definitions 2. Identifies examples in a literary selection 3. Uses the terms correctly in oral and written work	Encourage students to make a "literary dictionary" and to review the definitions periodically. Point out, and ask students to point out, examples during oral reading. Give oral and written assignments requiring use of the terms.	1. Short-answer test 2. Multiple-choice test 3. Observation and evaluation of written work
Interprets literary works 1. Identifies the major and minor themes 2. States the author's purpose or message 3. Identifies the tone and mood 4. Explains why the characters behave as they do 5. Points out specific parts of the literature that support the above interpretations 6. Relates the literary work to other writings	Read a brief literary work to class. Lead off discussion with questions concerning theme, author's purpose, tone, and character development. Analyze the parts of the literary work and show how they support the general interpretations. Generalize the method of analysis and interpretation by applying it to a second work. Have students select a literary work and write a critical analysis and interpretation.	Observation during class discussions. Objective test on specific points in a literary work and on the process of literary analysis. Essay questions calling for interpretations and supporting evidence. Evaluation of student's written reports (using criteria of effective interpretation).

Summary

Instructional objectives typically include some learning outcomes that can be considered minimum essentials and others that encourage the maximum development of the student. Both types should be considered when preparing a list of intended learning outcomes, and when teaching and testing.

1. Minimum essentials are typically low-level outcomes that are easily achieved by students and serve as prerequisites to further learning. The ability to add whole numbers, for example, is essential to solving word problems. Learning outcomes at the minimum-essential level are taught and tested directly on a one-to-one basis; that is, there is no variation between what is taught and what is tested.

2. Instructional objectives at the developmental level focus on students achieving the highest level of performance of which they are capable. Word problems involving mathematical reasoning, for example, can vary from simple problems that most students can solve to those so difficult that they can be solved by only a few. Learning outcomes at the developmental level are not taught and tested on a one-to-one basis. Instead, teaching is directed toward the general class of responses an

objective represents, and the test is based on a sample of the possible outcomes. An element of novelty is also typically introduced into the testing. Thus, a teacher may teach students strategies for solving mathematical reasoning problems, using various examples, but when tested the students will be asked to solve *new* problems. The test problems are also likely to vary in difficulty to determine the maximum level at which each student can perform.

3. Instructional objectives can aid in instructional planning if they are prepared first. This provides greater assurance that the methods and materials of instruction and the evaluation techniques are appropriate for the intended learning outcomes. An instructional planning chart may be useful as a guide.

Chapter 11

Using Instructional Objectives in Test Preparation

An achievement test is simply a device for obtaining a *sample* of student performance. For valid results, the sample must be in harmony with both the instructional objectives and the subject matter emphasized in the instruction. A satisfactory sample is most likely to be obtained when test preparation follows a systematic procedure. The following list of steps has been found to be useful for this purpose.

1. State the general instructional objectives and define each objective in terms of the specific types of performance students are expected to demonstrate at the end of instruction.
2. Make an outline of the content to be covered during the instruction.
3. Prepare a table of specifications that describes the nature of the test sample.
4. Construct test items that measure the sample of student performance specified in the table.

Each of these steps will be briefly described and illustrated for a unit in economics.

Defining the Objectives

Defining instructional objectives in terms of student performance serves two important purposes in test preparation: (1) It indicates the sample of specific learning outcomes that we are willing to accept as evidence that the objectives are being achieved, and (2) it specifies in precise terms the student performance that is to be measured by the test items. Because an achievement test is designed to measure a sample of student performance, it is important that the responses called forth by the test items be both relevant and representative.

These conditions would probably not be met without a carefully detailed description of the intended outcomes of instruction.

Following is a brief list of instructional objectives that has been defined by a list of specific learning outcomes. This list is for illustrative purposes only and therefore is not meant to be exhaustive; the list simply demonstrates the method of stating objectives for testing purposes.

OBJECTIVES FOR A UNIT IN ECONOMICS

1. Knows basic terms.

    1.1 Relates terms that have the same meaning.

    1.2 Selects the term that best fits a particular definition.

    1.3 Identifies terms used in reference to particular economic problems.

    1.4 Uses terms correctly in describing economic problems.

2. Understands economic concepts and principles.

    2.1 Identifies examples of economic concepts and principles.

    2.2 Describes economic concepts and principles in his own words.

    2.3 Identifies the interrelationship of economic principles.

    2.4 Explains changes in economic conditions in terms of the economic concepts and principles involved.

3. Applies economic principles to new situations.

    3.1 Identifies the economic principles needed to solve a practical problem.

    3.2 Predicts the probable outcome of an action involving economic principles.

    3.3 Describes how to solve a practical economic problem in terms of the economic principles involved.

    3.4 Distinguishes between probable and improbable economic forecasts.

4. Interprets economic data.

    4.1 Differentiates between relevant and irrelevant information.

    4.2 Differentiates between facts and inferences.

    4.3 Identifies cause–effect relations in data.

    4.4 Describes the trends in data.

    4.5 Distinguishes between warranted and unwarranted conclusions drawn from data.

    4.6 States proper qualifications when describing data.

Note that the statements of specific learning outcomes listed under each general objective describe how the students are expected to react toward the subject matter in economics but do not describe the specific subject matter toward which they are to react. Therefore, the specific statements listed under "Knows basic terms" describe what is meant by "knowing"—not what terms the students should know. Such statements make it possible to relate the objectives and the specific learning outcomes to various areas of content and thus to various units within the same course. As we shall see shortly, the table of specifications provides a method for relating the instructional objectives to the course content.

Outlining the Content

Because an achievement test should also adequately sample the subject matter included in the instruction, you should make an outline of the content to be covered by the test. The same content outline that is used for teaching may suffice, or a less elaborate outline may be developed as part of the test plan. The following list of topics for our illustrative unit in economics provides sufficient detail for testing purposes.

CONTENT OUTLINE FOR A UNIT IN ECONOMICS (MONEY AND BANKING)

A. Forms and functions of money.
   1. Types of money.
   2. Various uses of money.
B. Operation of banks.
   1. Services provided by commercial banks.
   2. Other institutions offering banking services.
   3. Role of banks in managing the flow of money.
C. Role of the Federal Reserve System.
   1. Need for flexibility in the money supply.
   2. Nature of the Federal Reserve System.
   3. Regulatory policies influencing the money supply.
D. State regulation of banks.
   1. The state banking commission.
   2. Laws to protect the borrowers.

The amount of detail to be included in the outline of content will, of course, depend on the length of time covered by the instruction. For a two-week unit of work, you may be able to include all of the major and minor topics. In outlining the content for an entire course, however, you may have to limit the outline to the main subject headings. Restricting the length of the outline to one or two pages is usually satisfactory for test-construction purposes.

Preparing the Table of Specifications

A table of specifications is a twofold table that relates the instructional objectives to the course content. The table makes it possible to classify each test item in terms of both objectives and content. A completed table describes the number of test items needed to obtain a balanced measure of the instructional objectives and the course content emphasized in the instruction.

A sample table of specifications, based on our illustrative unit in economics, is shown in Table X. To simplify the table, we have included only the general instructional objectives and major areas of content. This procedure is typical, although more detail may be desirable in some situations.

TABLE X. Table of Specifications for a 50-Item Test in Economics (Money and Banking)

	Instructional Objectives			
Content Areas	1 Knows Basic Terms	2 Understands Concepts and Principles	3 Applies Principles	4 Interprets Data
A. Forms and functions of money	3	4	3	
B. Operation of banks	4	3	5	3
C. Role of the Federal Reserve System	4	6	3	2
D. State regulation of banks	4	2	4	
Total number of test items	15	15	15	5

The numbers in each cell in the table indicate the number of test items to be constructed in each area. For example, there will be a total of 15 items that measure the objective "Knows basic terms"; 3 of these in the content area "Forms and functions of money," 4 of these in the content area "Operation of banks," and so on down the column. The total number of items in each column indicates the relative emphasis to be given to each objective, and the total number of items in each row indicates the relative emphasis to be given to each area of content. Therefore, the two-way grid specifies the test sample in terms of both instructional objectives and course content.

The relative emphasis shown in the table of specifications should, of course, reflect the emphasis given during instruction. This is accomplished by assigning weights to each objective and to each content area during the construction of the table. The usual procedure is first to distribute the total number (or percentage) of test items over the objectives and content areas and then to distribute the items among the individual cells. Although a number of factors might be considered in assigning such weights, the amount of instructional time devoted to each area will usually provide a satisfactory approximation. In Table X for instance, it is assumed that the *Interpretation of data* (5 test items) received only one third of the instructional emphasis given to each of the other objectives (15 test items each) and that this instruction was limited to content areas B and C. The table also indicates, by the number of items in each row, that content areas A and D received less instructional emphasis than areas B and C.

Constructing Relevant Test Items

The table of specifications describes the nature of the desired test sample and specifies what each test item should measure. The next task is to construct test items that are relevant to the instructional objectives and content areas of each cell. For example, in using Table X, let's assume that we are going to construct one of the four test items to measure the first objective ("Knows basic terms") in content area B ("Operation of banks"). Our procedure would be as follows: (1) to select one of the specific learning outcomes listed under the first objective, (2) to select one of the important banking terms, and (3) to construct a test item that calls forth the specific performance indicated in the learning outcome. Our test item should clearly reflect the desired learning outcome as follows:

Instructional Objective: 1. Knows basic terms.

Learning Outcome: 1.1 Relates terms that have the same meaning.

1. Checking accounts are also called

   *A. demand deposits.

   B. time deposits.

   C. currency.

   D. credit money.

Note in the above example that the learning outcome describes the specific response we expect the students to demonstrate and that the test item presents a relevant task. Other examples at the understanding and application levels are presented below. The objectives and outcomes are from our illustrative list of objectives for a unit in economics and are numbered accordingly.

Instructional Objective: 2. Understands economic concepts and principles.

Learning Outcome: 2.1 Identifies examples of economic concepts.

1. Which one of the following is an example of commercial credit?

   *A. A manufacturer borrows money to buy raw materials.

   B. A manufacturer borrows money to build a new plant.

   C. A business executive borrows money to build a new house.

   D. A stockbroker borrows money to buy stocks and bonds.

Instructional Objective: 3. Applies economic principles to new situations.

Learning Outcome: 3.2 Predicts the possible outcome of an action involving economic principles.

1. Which one of the following actions of the Federal Reserve Board would most likely contribute to greater inflation?

   *A. Buying government bonds on the open market.

   B. Raising the reserve requirments.

   C. Raising the discount rate.

   D. Lowering the amount of credit granted to member banks.

Specifications for Computer Item Banking

Some schools are now preparing pools of objectives and relevant test items for storage in a microcomputer. The items are coded by the specific learning outcome measured, content, grade level, and other relevant characteristics. When such item banks are stored,

* Correct answer.

the computer can be programmed to select items and build a test with known characteristics. The computer will print out these custom-designed tests and also provide scoring, reporting, and analyzing functions. The use of microcomputers in the school is relieving teachers of many of the time-consuming functions concerned with classroom testing.

A key feature of computer item banking is that *you get back only what you put in.* If you put in test items that are inappropriate for the objectives being measured or that are technically unsound, the printed test will provide an inadequate measure of the intended learning outcomes. Thus, it is especially important when developing an item bank to use detailed specifications for item writing. Examples of such specifications in several skill areas are presented in Boxes 11.1, 11.2, and 11.3.

Item banking is typically a cooperative affair among the teachers in a particular department. The detailed specifications provide greater assurance that a functionally equivalent set of relevant test items will be prepared for each specific learning outcome. The detail is also useful in clarifying the meaning of the test results during test interpretation.

BOX 11.1 READING

GENERAL INSTRUCTIONAL OBJECTIVE: Comprehends written material.
  SPECIFIC LEARNING OUTCOME: Identifies the main thought of a passage.
  TYPE OF TEST ITEMS: Multiple-choice (10 items).
  READING PASSAGE: One brief paragraph of material that is (1) of interest to children, and (2) at the sixth-grade reading level or lower.
  ITEM CHARACTERISTICS: Each test item will contain a stem in the form of a question or incomplete statement, followed by five alternative answers. The *stem* of the item will require the students to identify the main thought in the passage by selecting the word or phrase that best indicates the content of the passage. The *correct response* will be one that contains the central idea of the passage and incorporates the various details included in it. The *incorrect alternatives* (distracters) will contain ideas that are less important than the main thought. They will be made plausible by including content used in the passage and by matching the correct answer in terms of length and grammatical structure. The reading level of the item will be no higher than that of the passage.

Example

(Passage) The Koala is a cute, furry animal from Australia. Some of them live in the zoo in San Diego, California. They eat eucalyptus leaves and do not drink water. They are often called "koala bears" but they really aren't bears. They are marsupials, like the kangaroo.

Sample Item

This story is mostly about

    A. Australia
    B. bears
   *C. koalas
    D. marsupials

BOX 11.2 MATH

GENERAL INSTRUCTIONAL OBJECTIVE: Understands our number system.
  SPECIFIC LEARNING OUTCOME: Identifies place value.
  TYPE OF TEST ITEMS: Multiple-choice (10 items).
  ITEM CHARACTERISTICS: Each test item will contain a stem in the form of a question or incomplete statement, followed by four alternative answers. The *stem* of the item will contain a whole number with three to six digits. The student will be asked to identify the value of two of the digits by indicating the degree to which one is a multiple of the other. The *correct response* will indicate an understanding of the place value of both digits. The *incorrect alternatives* (distracters) will consist of common errors in identifying place value.

Sample Item

In the number 9,632, the 9 has a value that is

  A. three times the value of the 3
  B. thirty times the value of the 3
 *C. three hundred times the value of the 3
  D. three thousand times the value of the 3

The use of detailed specifications does not mean that the table of specifications, discussed earlier, is to be discarded. It can be used both in planning the overall structure of the item bank and in describing the make-up of the test that you want the computer to print for some particular use. In the later case, the table of specifications will help ensure that the printed test provides a balanced measure of the learning outcomes to be evaluated.

BOX 11.3 WRITING

GENERAL INSTRUCTIONAL OBJECTIVE: Knows fundamentals of written expression.
  SPECIFIC LEARNING OUTCOME: Distinguishes between complete and incomplete sentences.
  TYPE OF TEST ITEMS: Multiple-choice (10 items).
  ITEM CHARACTERISTICS: Each test item will contain one complete sentence and three incomplete sentences. The *stem* of the item will tell the student to choose the complete sentence. The *correct response* will be a complete sentence. The *incorrect alternatives* (distracters) will be sentence fragments.

Sample Item

Choose the *complete* sentence.

  A. The children who went to the zoo.
  B. The monkeys in the zoo swinging.
 *C. Going to the zoo was fun.
  D. Whatever you think of the zoo.

Summary

Instructional objectives play a key role in test preparation. They provide a description of the types of student performance we are willing to accept as evidence of achievement. We can construct a test that provides a relevant and representative measure of student performance by following these steps.

1. Clearly define the instructional objectives in terms of the specific learning outcomes that represent desired student performance.
2. Outline the content to be covered during the instruction.
3. Prepare a table of specifications that relates objectives and content and specifies the sample of test items to use.
4. Construct test items that call forth the desired student responses and matches the test sample specified in the table of specifications.

For computer item banking, it is desirable to use detailed specifications for item writing so that a set of functionally equivalent items can be prepared for each specific learning outcome.

For more elaborate descriptions and illustrations of how to prepare tables of specifications and how to construct test items that measure learning outcomes varying from simple to complex, see Gronlund and Linn (1990) and Gronlund (1988) in the list of references in Appendix C.

Chapter 12

Using Instructional Objectives in Preparing Evaluation Instruments

There are a number of learning outcomes that cannot be measured by the traditional paper and pencil test. Most of these fall in the area of affective outcomes (e.g., attitudes, social relations) and performance outcomes (e.g., speaking, laboratory skill). In evaluating these types of learning outcomes, we need to depend more heavily on observation and self-report methods. In evaluating some performance skills, for example, we need to observe the ongoing performance and check whether the proper procedures were followed (e.g., using a checklist), or judge the effectiveness of the performance (e.g., using a rating scale). If a product is involved, such as a theme or woodworking project, performance skill can also be evaluated by judging the quality of the product (e.g., using a rating scale). In evaluating affective outcomes, such as the ability to get along with others, we need to observe students in a variety of situations and judge (e.g., rate) their effectiveness in social relations. In some cases, for example in evaluating attitudes, we may also want to have students indicate on a self-report instrument how they feel about school, a particular course, or some activity (e.g., using an attitude scale). Thus, both observational instruments and self-report methods can play an important role in evaluating those outcomes that cannot be measured by the usual paper-and-pencil test.

As with testing procedures, the instructional objectives provide the guidelines for preparing appropriate evaluation techniques. If the specific learning outcomes have been carefully written for performance or affective outcomes, they can be easily converted to a rating scale, checklist, or self-report form for use in evaluation. In this chapter we shall briefly describe and illustrate these methods.

Rating Scales

The rating scale provides a convenient observational guide. It (1) focuses attention on the specific performance or behavior to be observed, and (2) provides a convenient method for recording the judgments of the observer. Typically, the rating scale can be easily prepared by using the specific learning outcomes as the items to be observed and adding a scale for rating on each item.

Let's assume that the following performance objective and set of specific learning outcomes have been specified for a science course (taken from Chapter 8).

1. Uses laboratory equipment properly.
   1.1 Selects appropriate equipment for an experiment.
   1.2 Assembles equipment correctly for the experiment.
   1.3 Manipulates equipment as needed during the experiment.
   1.4 Measures accurately with proper measuring device.
   1.5 Follows safety rules in conducting experiment.
   1.6 Uses materials without wasting any.
   1.7 Completes experiment within time limits.
   1.8 Cleans equipment and returns to proper place.

Each of these specific learning outcomes can serve as an item in a rating scale by simply modifying the wording slightly and by adding a place beneath each item to record the ratings, as shown in Figure 1.

The complete rating scale would, of course, include (1) items covering all specific outcomes to be evaluated, (2) directions for making the ratings, and (3) possibly a place for comments beneath each rating scale item. All we are doing here is illustrating how easy it is to construct a rating scale when the intended outcomes have been clearly specified. The specific learning outcomes indicate the performance to be observed and, thus, become the items in the rating instrument. The graphic scale beneath each item simply provides a place to record the ratings. Using both numbers and descriptive statements to define the points on the scale makes the rating task easier and aids in the interpretation of results.

The same procedure used for preparing a performance rating scale can be used for affective outcomes, as illustrated in Figure 2. Note that the item in each area is derived directly from the specific learning outcome. Thus, the key element in preparing a rating scale for either performance or affective evaluation is a clearly stated set of intended outcomes. It is then simply a matter of converting each outcome to a rating scale item and adding a graphic scale beneath it for a place to record the rating.

Checklists

Like the rating scale, the checklist (1) directs attention to the performance to be observed, and (2) provides a convenient method of recording observations. The main difference between them is in the type of judgment to be made. The rating scale calls for a judgment concerning the degree to which a characteristic is present, whereas the checklist calls for a yes–no response. Thus, it is used to indicate whether a characteristic is present or absent or whether a proper action was taken.

The construction of a checklist, like other evaluation techniques, is derived directly from the set of specific learning outcomes. In this case it is simply a matter of listing the

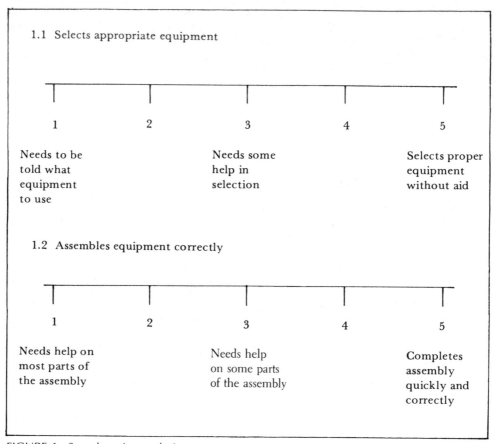

FIGURE 1. Sample rating scale items.

intended outcomes and providing a place to check yes or no. The checklist in Figure 3 is derived from an illustrative list of affective outcomes presented in Chapter 7. These same items could also be used in a rating scale, of course, if *degree* of class participation is desired. The advantage of the checklist is the ease of preparation and the ease of recording observations.

A checklist is also useful for evaluating whether each step in a procedure has been properly performed. For this type evaluation, we need a description of each step and a place to mark whether or not the performance was satisfactory. An illustrative checklist for evaluating the application of varnish is shown in Figure 4. The items in this checklist are from an illustrative, performance objective in Chapter 8. Note that the specific tasks have been placed in the approximate order in which they are to be performed. The observer then simply has to check whether each completed step was satisfactory or un-satisfactory. This type of judgment does not, of course, provide for degrees of proficiency in performing the task. It simply indicates whether each step was taken and whether the performance was acceptable. To describe levels of proficiency beyond the acceptable minimum we would need a more detailed rating system, such as the 5-point scale illustrated earlier.

WORK HABITS

Specific Learning Outcome: Follows instructions in attempting new task.

Rating Scale Item:

How well does individual follow instructions?

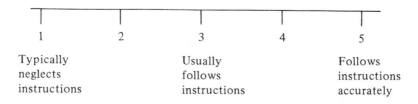

1	2	3	4	5
Typically neglects instructions		Usually follows instructions		Follows instructions accurately

SOCIAL RELATIONSHIPS

Specific Learning Outcome: Relates well to others.

Rating Scale Item:

How well does individual get along with others?

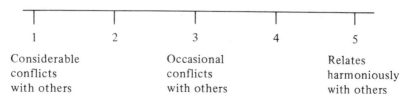

1	2	3	4	5
Considerable conflicts with others		Occasional conflicts with others		Relates harmoniously with others

CONCERN FOR OTHERS

Specific Learning Outcome: Shares ideas and materials willingly.

Rating Scale Item:

Willingness to share ideas and materials.

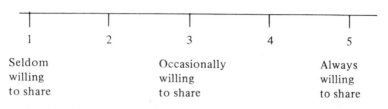

1	2	3	4	5
Seldom willing to share		Occasionally willing to share		Always willing to share

FIGURE 2. Sample rating scale items for evaluating specific outcomes in various affective areas.

PARTICIPATION IN CLASSROOM ACTIVITIES

Directions: Circle YES or NO to indicate your response.

YES   NO   1. Listens attentively.
YES   NO   2. Asks relevant questions.
YES   NO   3. Participates in classroom discussions.
YES   NO   4. Volunteers for special tasks.
YES   NO   5. Contributes material for the bulletin board.
YES   NO   6. Helps others when requested.

FIGURE 3. Checklist for evaluating class participation.

Some performance outcomes require evaluation of both the procedure and the product. In this case, both can be included on a single evaluation form and the approach is still the same. The specific learning outcomes specify what elements of the procedure and the product are to be observed, and the checklist or rating scale merely provides a convenient method of recording our judgments.

DIRECTIONS: On the space in front of each item, place a plus (+) sign if performance was satisfactory, place a minus (−) sign if it was unsatisfactory.

_____   1. Sands and prepares surface properly.

_____   2. Wipes dust from surface with appropriate cloth.

_____   3. Selects appropriate brush.

_____   4. Selects varnish and checks varnish flow.

_____   5. Pours needed amount of varnish into clean container.

_____   6. Puts brush properly into varnish (1/3 of bristle length).

_____   7. Wipes excess varnish from brush on inside edge of container.

_____   8. Applies varnish to surface with smooth strokes.

_____   9. Works from center of surface toward the edges.

_____   10. Brushes with the grain of the wood.

_____   11. Uses light strokes to smooth the varnish.

_____   12. Checks surface for completeness.

_____   13. Cleans brush with appropriate cleaner.

_____   14. Does *not* pour excess varnish back into can.

_____   15. Cleans work area.

FIGURE 4. Checklist for evaluating the proper application of varnish.

Self-Report Method

Some affective outcomes are concerned with students' inner feelings that cannot be evaluated by observation alone. Probably the most educationally significant of those is attitude; for example, attitude toward school, attitude toward a particular course, or attitude toward some activity. Although some information concerning attitude can be gleaned from observation, overt behavior is not a dependable indicator of inner feelings. Thus, observation needs to be supplemented by an individual's own report about how he feels. Self-report instruments are frequently used for this purpose.

The self-report device most widely used by teachers is probably the attitude scale. There are various methods for preparing attitude scales, but one of the simplest is the Likert method. This involves just two basic steps. (1) Select clearly favorable and clearly unfavorable attitude statements. (2) Provide for responses on the following 5-point scale; strongly agree (SA), agree (A), undecided (U), disagree (D), and strongly disagree (SD). An illustrative Likert-type scale for attitude toward a science course is shown in Figure 5.

In scoring favorable statements, like the first item in Figure 5, the five alternatives are given values of 5, 4, 3, 2, 1, going from SA to SD. In scoring unfavorable statements, like the second item in Figure 5, these values are reversed. Thus, they are given values of 1, 2, 3, 4, 5, going from SA to SD. An individual's score on this type of scale is the sum of the scores on all items, with a higher score indicating a more favorable attitude.

Directions: Indicate how much you agree or disagree with each statement by circling the appropriate letter(s).

		KEY			SA — Strongly Agree A — Agree U — Undecided D — Disagree SD — Strongly Disagree

SA	A	U	D	SD	1. Science classes are interesting.
SA	A	U	D	SD	2. Science laboratory is dull and boring.
SA	A	U	D	SD	3. It is fun working on science problems.
SA	A	U	D	SD	4. Class activities are good.
SA	A	U	D	SD	5. Reading the textbook is a waste of time.
SA	A	U	D	SD	6. The laboratory experiments are interesting.
SA	A	U	D	SD	7. Most class activities are monotonous.
SA	A	U	D	SD	8. I enjoy reading the textbook.
SA	A	U	D	SD	9. The problems we are studying are unimportant.
SA	A	U	D	SD	10. I am *not* very enthusiastic about science.

FIGURE 5. Illustrative Likert-type attitude scale for measuring attitude toward a science course. (Reprinted from Gronlund, N. E. and Linn, R. L., *Measurement and Evaluation in Teaching,* 6th ed., New York, Macmillan, 1990. Used by permission.)

As with other evaluation techniques, the self-report method should be prepared in harmony with the outcomes to be evaluated. For example, describing in specific terms what is meant by a "favorable attitude toward science" provides the basis for selecting statements that are clearly favorable and clearly unfavorable. It is then simply a matter of adding the 5-point scale to each item and including directions that tell the students how to respond.

Summary

Learning outcomes in the affective and performance areas are typically evaluated by some type of observational or self-report device. Three of the most commonly used techniques are the rating scale, checklist, and attitude scale. As with testing procedures, the instructional objectives provide the guidelines for preparing each of these instruments.

1. A rating scale can be prepared by listing the specific learning outcomes as items to be observed and adding a scale for rating on each item. Thus, it focuses attention on the performance or behavior to be observed and provides a convenient method for recording judgments.

2. A checklist is used to indicate whether a characteristic is present or absent or whether a proper action was taken. Like the rating scale, it consists of a list of specific learning outcomes, but here the observer simply checks one of two categories, such as present–absent, yes–no, or satisfactory–unsatisfactory.

3. A self-report method is used to obtain information concerning inner feelings. Probably the most widely used self-report device by teachers is the attitude scale. This consists of a list containing favorable and unfavorable statements with a scale for reporting degrees of agreement or disagreement with each statement. As with other evaluation techniques, the statements should be in harmony with the outcomes to be evaluated.

In this chapter, we have been simply attempting to show how evaluation instruments are derived directly from instructional objectives and the list of specific learning outcomes that define them. More detailed descriptions of observational techniques and self-report methods can be found in Gronlund and Linn (1990), and attitude scale construction is described and illustrated in Mueller (1986). See references in Appendix C.

Appendix A

Checklist for Evaluating the Final List of Objectives

In this book we have described and illustrated how to identify and define instructional objectives in terms of student performance. Our focus was on the *stating* of the objectives and the specific learning outcomes. Questions such as "Which objectives are most desirable for a particular instructional unit?" we leave to the curriculum specialist and subject expert. In evaluating your final list of objectives, however, you might want to appraise the adequacy of the list, as well as how clearly the statements indicate your instructional intent. Therefore, general criteria for evaluating the final list of objectives and specific learning outcomes have been incorporated into this checklist.

The checklist is intended as a diagnostic tool for detecting and correcting errors in the final list of objectives. Any negative answer indicates an area where improvement is needed. The checklist is also useful, of course, as a guide for developing the original list of instructional objectives.

Checklist

	Yes	No

Adequacy of the List of General Instructional Objectives

1. Does each general instructional objective indicate an appropriate outcome for the instructional unit? (See recommendations of curriculum and subject experts.) _____ _____
2. Does the list of general instructional objectives include all logical outcomes of the unit (knowledge, understanding, skills, attitudes, etc.)? _____ _____

97

	Yes	No

3. Are the general instructional objectives attainable (do they take into account the ability of the students, facilities, time available, etc.)? _____ _____

4. Are the general instructional objectives in harmony with the philosophy of the school? _____ _____

5. Are the general instructional objectives in harmony with sound principles of learning (e.g., are the outcomes those that are most permanent and transferrable)? _____ _____

Statements of General Instructional Objectives

6. Does each general instructional objective begin with a *verb* (e.g., knows, understands, appreciates)? _____ _____

7. Is each general instructional objective stated in terms of *student performance* (rather than teacher performance)? _____ _____

8. Is each general instructional objective stated as a learning product (rather than in terms of the learning process)? _____ _____

9. Is each general instructional objective stated in terms of the students' *terminal performance* (rather than the subject matter to be covered)? _____ _____

10. Does each general instructional objective include only one general learning outcome? _____ _____

11. Is each general instructional objective stated at the proper level of generality (i.e., is it clear, concise, and readily definable)? _____ _____

12. Is each general instructional objective stated so that it is relatively independent (i.e., free from overlap with other objectives)? _____ _____

Statements of Specific Learning Outcomes

13. Is each general instructional objective defined by a list of specific learning outcomes that describes the types of performance students are expected to demonstrate? _____ _____

14. Does each specific learning outcome begin with a *verb* that specifies definite, *observable performance* (e.g., identifies, describes, lists)? _____ _____

15. Is the performance described in each specific learning outcome relevant to the general instructional objective? _____ _____

	Yes	No

16. Is there a sufficient number of specific learning outcomes to describe adequately the performance of students who have achieved each of the general instructional objectives? _____ _____

17. Is each specific learning outcome sufficiently free of course content so that it can be used with various units of study? _____ _____

Appendix B

Illustrative Verbs

Illustrative Verbs for Stating General Instructional Objectives

Analyze	Compute	Interpret	Perform	Translate
Apply	Create	Know	Recognize	Understand
Appreciate	Demonstrate	Listen	Speak	Use
Comprehend	Evaluate	Locate	Think	Write

Illustrative Verbs for Stating Specific Learning Outcomes[1]

"CREATIVE" BEHAVIORS

Alter	Paraphrase	Reconstruct	Rephrase	Rewrite
Ask	Predict	Regroup	Restate	Simplify
Change	Question	Rename	Restructure	Synthesize
Design	Rearrange	Reorder	Retell	Systematize
Generalize	Recombine	Reorganize	Revise	Vary
Modify				

COMPLEX, LOGICAL, JUDGMENTAL BEHAVIORS

Analyze	Conclude	Deduce	Formulate	Plan
Appraise	Contrast	Defend	Generate	Structure
Combine	Criticize	Evaluate	Induce	Substitute
Compare	Decide	Explain	Infer	

[1] This list was developed by Calvin K. Claus, Psychology Department, National College of Education, Evanston, Ill. Printed by permission from a paper presented at the annual meeting of the National Council on Measurement in Education (Chicago: February, 1968). It provides a useful collection of verbs for the beginner.

GENERAL DISCRIMINATIVE BEHAVIORS

Choose	Detect	Identify	Match	Place
Collect	Differentiate	Indicate	Omit	Point
Define	Discriminate	Isolate	Order	Select
Describe	Distinguish	List	Pick	Separate

SOCIAL BEHAVIORS

Accept	Communicate	Discuss	Invite	Praise
Agree	Compliment	Excuse	Join	React
Aid	Contribute	Forgive	Laugh	Smile
Allow	Cooperate	Greet	Meet	Talk
Answer	Dance	Help	Participate	Thank
Argue	Disagree	Interact	Permit	Volunteer

LANGUAGE BEHAVIORS

Abbreviate	Edit	Punctuate	Speak	Tell
Accent	Hyphenate	Read	Spell	Translate
Alphabetize	Indent	Recite	State	Verbalize
Articulate	Outline	Say	Summarize	Whisper
Call	Print	Sign	Syllabify	Write
Capitalize	Pronounce			

"STUDY" BEHAVIORS

Arrange	Compile	Itemize	Mark	Record
Categorize	Copy	Label	Name	Reproduce
Chart	Diagram	Locate	Note	Search
Circle	Find	Look	Organize	Sort
Cite	Follow	Map	Quote	Underline

MUSIC BEHAVIORS

Blow	Compose	Hum	Pluck	Strum
Bow	Finger	Mute	Practice	Tap
Clap	Harmonize	Play	Sing	Whistle

PHYSICAL BEHAVIORS

Arch	Chase	Grasp	Kick	Pull
Bat	Climb	Grip	Knock	Push
Bend	Face	Hit	Lift	Run
Carry	Float	Hop	March	Skate
Catch	Grab	Jump	Pitch	Ski

Appendix B

| Skip | Stand | Stretch | Swing | Toss |
| Somersault | Step | Swim | Throw | Walk |

ARTS BEHAVIORS

Assemble	Dot	Illustrate	Press	Stamp
Blend	Draw	Melt	Roll	Stick
Brush	Drill	Mix	Rub	Stir
Build	Fold	Mold	Sand	Trace
Carve	Form	Nail	Saw	Trim
Color	Frame	Paint	Sculpt	Varnish
Construct	Hammer	Paste	Shake	Wipe
Cut	Handle	Pat	Sketch	Wrap
Dab	Heat	Pour	Smooth	

DRAMA BEHAVIORS

Act	Display	Express	Pass	Show
Clasp	Emit	Leave	Perform	Sit
Cross	Enter	Move	Proceed	Start
Direct	Exit	Pantomime	Respond	Turn

MATHEMATICAL BEHAVIORS

Add	Derive	Group	Number	Square
Bisect	Divide	Integrate	Plot	Subtract
Calculate	Estimate	Interpolate	Prove	Tabulate
Check	Extrapolate	Measure	Reduce	Tally
Compute	Extract	Multiply	Solve	Verify
Count	Graph			

LABORATORY SCIENCE BEHAVIORS

Apply	Demonstrate	Keep	Prepare	Specify
Calibrate	Dissect	Lengthen	Remove	Straighten
Conduct	Feed	Limit	Replace	Time
Connect	Grow	Manipulate	Report	Transfer
Convert	Increase	Operate	Reset	Weigh
Decrease	Insert	Plant	Set	

GENERAL APPEARANCE, HEALTH, AND SAFETY BEHAVIORS

Button	Close	Dress	Eliminate	Fill
Clean	Comb	Drink	Empty	Go
Clear	Cover	Eat	Fasten	Lace

Stop	Unbutton	Untie	Wait	Wear
Taste	Uncover	Unzip	Wash	Zip
Tie				

MISCELLANEOUS

Aim	Erase	Lead	Relate	Stake
Attempt	Expand	Lend	Repeat	Start
Attend	Extend	Let	Return	Stock
Begin	Feel	Light	Ride	Store
Bring	Finish	Make	Rip	Strike
Buy	Fit	Mend	Save	Suggest
Come	Fix	Miss	Scratch	Supply
Complete	Flip	Offer	Send	Support
Consider	Get	Open	Serve	Switch
Correct	Give	Pack	Sew	Take
Crease	Grind	Pay	Share	Tear
Crush	Guide	Peel	Sharpen	Touch
Designate	Hand	Pin	Shoot	Try
Determine	Hang	Position	Shorten	Twist
Develop	Hold	Present	Shovel	Type
Discover	Hook	Produce	Shut	Use
Distribute	Hunt	Propose	Signify	Vote
Do	Include	Provide	Slide	Watch
Drop	Inform	Put	Slip	Weave
End	Lay	Raise	Spread	Work

Appendix C

References

BLOOM, B. S., ed., et al. *Taxonomy of Educational Objectives: Handbook I, Cognitive Domain*. New York: David McKay Co., Inc., 1956. Describes the cognitive categories in detail and presents illustrative objectives and test items for each.

GRONLUND, N. E. *How to Construct Achievement Tests*, 4th ed. Englewood Cliffs, N.J.: Prentice Hall, Inc., 1988. Describes and illustrates how to construct test items that measure learning outcomes at various levels.

GRONLUND, N. E. AND LINN, R. L. *Measurement and Evaluation in Teaching*, 6th ed. New York: Macmillan Publishing Co., Inc., 1990. A textbook that describes the process of preparing instructional objectives and using them in testing and evaluating student learning.

HARROW, A. J. A *Taxonomy of the Psychomotor Domain*. New York: David McKay Co., Inc., 1972. Provides a model for classifying learning outcomes in the psychomotor domain and presents illustrative objectives.

KRATHWOHL, D. R., ed., et al. *Taxonomy of Educational Objectives: Handbook II, Affective Domain*. New York: David McKay Co., Inc., 1964. Describes the affective categories in detail and presents illustrative objectives and test items for each.

MARZANO, R. J., et al. *Dimensions of Thinking*: A Framework for Curriculum and Instruction, Association for Supervision and Curriculum Development, Alexandria, Virginia, 1988.

MUELLER, D. J. *Measuring Social Attitudes*. New York: Teachers College Press, 1986. Describes and illustrates how to construct attitude scales.

SIMPSON, E. J. "The Classification of Educational Objectives in the Psychomotor Domain." *The Psychomotor Domain*. Vol. 3. Washington: Gryphon House, 1972. Describes the psychomotor domain in detail and presents illustrative objectives.

Index